Between
Faith
and
Doubt

Between
Faith
and
Doubt

An Evolving Faith Journey

Samuel Cardillo

BETWEEN FAITH AND DOUBT: AN EVOLVING FAITH JOURNEY

1405 SW 6th Avenue • Ocala, Florida 34471 • Phone 352-622-1825 • Fax 352-622-1875
Website: www.atlantic-pub.com • Email: sales@atlantic-pub.com
SAN Number: 268-1250

Library of Congress Control Number: 2020917914

Printed in the United States

PROJECT MANAGER: Crystal Edwards
INTERIOR LAYOUT AND JACKET DESIGN: Nicole Sturk

Contents

Preface: The Enigma of Faith..1

Introduction: Why I Wrote This Book 7
   Reason One: To Describe A Faith Journey In Progress.....................7
   Reason Two: To Address Conflicting Images Of God 11

Part One: Setting Out on a Faith Journey 17
   The Risk, Power, And Mystery Of Faith 18
   Some Questions About A Faith Journey 36

Part Two: My Faith Journey 57
   The Risk of Openness About a Faith Journey 58
   Desiring Faith versus Having Faith...60
   The Problem Of Relating to a "Hidden" God..............................61
   The Phases of My Faith Journey 66
   The Main Point: Fighting The War Against Doubt......................84

Part Three: Journey Toward Faith 91
   Questioning Foundations Of The Faith......................................92
   Mystery Versus Contradiction: More Questions Than Answers......103
   Faith, Sovereignty, And Free Will 111

Is Faith Trust Or Belief?..124

Faith And Scholarship 127

Faith And Exclusivity 132

Paul's Misapplication Of Old Testament Scripture..........141

Faith Journey Through Later Life 146

The Strongest Argument For Faith And Hope 150

The Journey Continues..154

Conclusion..157

Selected Writings 161

Bibliography 173

The Enigma of Faith

In *The Hobbit,* J. R. R. Tolkien's famous prequel to *The Lord of the Rings,* we're introduced to Bilbo Baggins, a self-absorbed and contented Hobbit living a life of ease in the Shire with no serious obligations. When he is suddenly faced with the challenge to embark on an adventure with a band of Dwarfs set on recovering their stolen treasure, he is reluctant to leave the comfort of the Shire and go along on this dangerous quest. After all, it wasn't his treasure they were after, and he was quite happy with things the way they were.

The opening scene is, as Tolkien described it, an "unexpected party" as the 13 dwarfs intrude, one by one, on Bilbo's serene existence. Bilbo, who we see as timid and seemingly uninterested in anything beyond his next meal, gradually recognizes his own need to go on the adventure and steps out in what is certainly an act of faith. While somewhat reluctant at first, he goes, not knowing the danger and thrill of what lies ahead on the journey—only that he is compelled to act.

After Bilbo's journey (related at the end of *The Hobbit* and in *The Lord of the Rings*), when he is old and gray, we see how much he has changed in his attitude toward adventure. He who (as a young Hobbit) had said to Gandalf in that opening scene, "Sorry, I don't want any adventures, thank you. Not today . . ." now reflects on his life and says, "This is a bitter adventure, if it must end so; and not a mountain of gold can amend it. *Yet I am glad that I have shared in your perils—that has been more than any Baggins deserves."*

In one way, life consists of a series of adventures—occasions that challenge us to step out of our comfort zone and explore something beyond what has become the "usual" for us. The temptation is to stay in the comfort of what we are used to; to avoid stepping out beyond our self-imposed limitations because venturing out into the unknown can be frightening, not to mention dangerous. Much like Bilbo Baggins, I've come to the place where the idea of stepping out of what has always been the safety and certainty of my comfort zone has become a challenge that is increasingly impossible to ignore. Maybe it's just midlife crisis (a little late perhaps, since I'm now in my 60s). But whatever it is, the urge doesn't go away. I'm compelled to keep moving forward, one step at a time, reluctantly and fearfully at certain points, but with a sure conviction that the only proper course of action is to continue on the path. As I'll relate in this book, my journey is a journey of faith.

Having spent my entire life as a practicing Christian, my world has been characterized by the conviction to live a life of faithfulness to the Christian foundations into which I was born and in which I have been immersed my whole life. But those foundations have been shaken in recent years. This book is an account of what that shaking looks like, how it has developed into a faith crisis, and how it has shaped my thinking as I've worked to navigate through it and resolve it.

* * *

While lying awake in the middle of the night recently, trying to capture my scattered and fleeting thoughts, in that half-asleep, half-awake state, it occurred to me that I was at a point in my life toward which I had been heading for some time, but the progress of which I had been resisting. It felt like I was more or less midway through a battle for my faith, halfway in and halfway out, between faith and doubt, in that no-man's land that can perhaps best be described as a place of uncertainty; wondering if I could (or should) somehow try to salvage and reignite my dying faith, to go on trying to keep my head above water while moving toward what felt more and more like the deep and dangerous end of the pool. It's an uncomfortable but unavoidable place.

I've gone through periods of doubt before, and, in fact, I believe it's a fairly common experience among others in the world of evangelical Christianity. But those periods were relatively short-lived and resolved rather easily and quickly. This battle is different. It's been raging for a few years, and it has taken on a steadily increasing intensity. The battle feels something like this: Your instinct tells you to get past the doubt, to stick with your faith because it's all you've known for most of your life, and it's always been a safe and comfortable place—safe because of the fear of consequences for giving it up, and comfortable because of the support system that has been built up around you to sustain it. But at the same time, for a variety of reasons, you're simply not as convinced about its merit and verifiability as you used to be because for the most part, over time, much of it has ceased to make sense to the intellect. As a result, it has become a matter of the very survival of your faith.

There could be any number of reasons why your quest for faith has become a battleground, and I'll explore those reasons. But in many cases, for me at least, the underlying rationale is simply that while my faith continues to struggle to stay alive, in many ways it has ceased to be a meaningful spiritual or intellectual pursuit. Some might argue that the essence of faith is, above all, a spiritual connection that can only truly be made apart from the intellect or that faith shouldn't be judged as to its appeal to the intellect. As Victor Frankl put it, "Feeling can be much more sensitive than reason can ever be sensible." He expands on that idea when he writes, "Sometimes the wisdom of our hearts proves to be deeper than the insight of our brains. And sometimes the most reasonable thing is not to try to be too reasonable."[1] There's merit to that idea of course. As Pascal famously said it, "The heart has its reasons that reason knows nothing of." In the simple words of that surprising sage Napoleon Dynamite: "Just listen to your heart." Sound

---

1. Viktor Frankl, *The Will to Meaning* (New York: Penguin Books, 1969), page 95.

advice, of course, to an extent. But our capacity and inclination to reason isn't a choice that we make; we are no less thinking and reasoning beings than we are spiritual beings. Therefore, a proposition, such as the merit of faith, must pass through the intellect in order to be adopted as valid. When a proposition loses its appeal to our intellect, no matter how much wishful thinking would prompt us to hold on to it, the value of that proposition can only weaken, and therefore diminish, in its appeal to the sensibility.

The point is that it happens—different ideas appeal to us and captivate us at certain points in life for whatever reasons, but the circumstances of life sometimes change so drastically as to prompt a reevaluation of our most fundamental certainties. And whether that happens suddenly or over a period of time, its progression to the point of crisis is unexpected. In the midst of the battle, the urge is to ignore or accept as normal the feeling that you're in a persistent wrestling match with an elusive foe, who you know you're supposed to be able to defeat because you have all the right counter-measures (or in this case, the right resources at your disposal). After all, this isn't the first time you've wrestled with your faith.

I've not verified this, but I would guess that every serious Christian experiences periods of questioning, whether short-lived and quickly overcome or drawn out over a long period of time. It's the nature of faith for individuals to periodically experience the cycle of weakness and restoration. But this battle is different. In this battle your opponent, doubt, refuses to give in, so the fight lingers on—like Jacob's wrestling match with God in Genesis 32. Sometimes the urge is to shout, like Jacob, "I won't let you go until you bless me!" or, in my case, "I won't stop wrestling through this doubt until you convince me otherwise!" You live with a profound sense that your commitment to the faith is too important to give up, but at the same time, you're worn out and just want to end the fight, to call it a draw, to realize that there'll be no winner and move on to that in-between state, which I would call nominal faith (faith in name only).

During that restless night, the phrase "understanding seeking faith" came to mind, and I remembered it was the title of a book that had caught my attention years ago. The phrase captures exactly what I've been thinking and feeling lately. This book is an attempt to understand how and why the faith that rather comfortably sustained me through the first 60 years of my life has become elusive, hidden, and needing to be sought out in fresh ways, dying and needing to be resuscitated. It feels very much like a battle for the survival of that faith. I hesitate to use the language of "survival" because it seems ominous, but it's not an exaggeration to say that I truly feel like I'm fighting for the survival of my faith. So often that fight takes the form of the question, "Is it worth fighting for?" I think the fact that I haven't given up yet proves that it very well might be. To be honest, I'm not completely sure at this point. But that question is a key factor underlying the reason I wrote this book. So my purpose is to both *understand* and *seek out* a true reality of that faith that once was unquestioned … or to concede the battle and give it all up. So, with all of the uncertainty, I am sure of one thing: This questioning can't be wished away as if it didn't exist; it can't be minimized or put off to a more convenient time; it can't be ignored; it simply can't be avoided. It is a head-on battle.

Defining faith

Try to define faith. It can take you in so many different directions. Is faith a possession? A set of values that you strive to live by? Adherence to a set of religious beliefs? Assurance of some truth proposition? Commitment to live a certain way?

As a general starting point toward comprehending the phenomenon, broadly speaking, I would propose that faith is both a battle and a journey. It's a battle because it's not easily won. I would suggest that anyone who tells you otherwise hasn't yet had their faith challenged to any serious degree—to the point of a faith crisis. But faith is also a journey because it takes a lifetime, at the very least, to get hold of it. If you're honest with yourself, you'll recognize that deep down inside, in that place where no one goes but you, questions about your faith arise from time to time. If you're even more honest, questions about your faith might be a persistent part of your life. If, even in a fleeting moment of retrospection, an occasional suspicion about the validity of your faith has crossed your mind, you have questioned your faith. The point is, it's a common experience. In fact, it's okay because it's honest.

In Part One, I'll talk about how faith is defined in the New Testament's famous chapter on faith (Hebrews chapter 11). But for now, I'll just point out that in everyday conversation, faith is defined in the sense that I indicated above: as something you "have" or don't have; a possession that, once you have it, is yours to keep or let go of, like a gift or any other possession you come in to. "Have faith," someone might say to you. "*Ok, thanks, I'll take it.*" If only it were that simple. Faith is also described by its degree of power or intensity ("Is your faith strong or weak?") or your degree of conviction or assurance about it ("How certain are you about your faith?"). It's sometimes defined as a condition or a state of being that you are "in" at any given time ("Are you living in faith or in doubt?"). And faith is usually quantified ("How much faith do you have?") as if the amount of faith you possess could determine the extent of your success or failure in any given venture in life or as if your faith were a currency that you could exchange for some spiritual benefit in return. On one occasion Jesus said to his followers, "If you have faith and do not doubt . . . even if you say to this mountain, 'Be lifted up and thrown into the sea,' it will happen" (Matthew 21:21). Really? To my knowledge, no one has ever successfully tested that challenge. I wonder why . . . Finally, faith is sometimes defined as something you can lose or misplace: "Where's your faith?"

INTRODUCTION

Why I Wrote This Book

S ince the mystery of faith has been one of my life's biggest and most persistent challenges, I decided to explore the phenomenon of faith (or lack thereof) in my own life openly and honestly, asking questions that have for a long time been brewing inside, but until now I've avoided probing for fear of what I might discover, or perhaps for fear of what I might reveal about myself. With that as background, I've written this book for two reasons that might seem to be unrelated on the surface but in fact thoroughly interrelate.

Reason One: To Describe A Faith Journey In Progress

First, I wanted to show what a faith journey looks like in midprogress— that is, from the point of view of someone who has not yet navigated his way to the end of that journey. Why? Typically, we read about the lives of people who have fought through a spiritual crisis *after* they've come through it and emerged into a restored or more robust faith. But in so doing, we don't gain a real-time sense of the experience of going through the crisis; rather, we're guided past the crisis to the resolution and therefore fail to gain a sense of the vital lessons learned along the way—lessons that can only truly be learned firsthand. As Rachel Evans put it, "Church books are written by people with a plan and 10 steps, not by Christians just hanging on by their fingernails." A quick Amazon search for books about faith crises brings up books with advertising blurbs like these:

"... will enable you to not just 'manage' but to overcome all the obstacles in your path."

"... how to overcome any crisis by applying the sure wisdom and the time-tested principles of the Kingdom of God."

"... how the greatest men of the Bible came through their own time of crisis with victory by allowing God to fight their battles for them."

Desperation is a dangerous but common motivation for trying to fix one's spiritual condition. I know this quite well from experience. Too many times in my spiritual journey, I settled on the same old body of belief just to find relief from the turmoil of uncertainty, or of not being "in sync" with a community of like-minded people who seem to "get it" and who never seem to struggle with uncertainty. Not being confident about what you believe is extremely uncomfortable when those in your religious circle are beyond that (or at least act as if they are). That's why I insist on slowing down and taking doubt seriously. If you're looking for quick answers that have helped other people who have gone through spiritual hard times, those "how to" books might serve their purpose for you. But if you find yourself in a place where the answers that have apparently helped some people walk through dark times have been for you too superficial or unconvincing or simply don't resonate for whatever reason, I would suggest that you set out on your own journey to navigate your way through your crisis. Reading encouraging books written by other people about their own success might give you partial or temporary help through your struggle. But you won't find real, permanent solutions by reading about how someone else overcame through their journey because your life is unique and the circumstances of your journey are uniquely yours.

I would suggest that what you need most when you are in the middle of your faith crisis, first and foremost, is to not rush through it to get "back on track," to not push it aside as an anomaly in your life, to not rationalize it away as some sort of negative experience that isn't supposed to happen to a solid and well-grounded Christian like you, but, rather, to take ownership of what you're going through. Don't be ashamed about it, but, instead, recognize it as a predictable outcome of who you are as a thoughtful human being. Embrace it, nourish it, dig deep into its roots, and absorb all that it brings to the surface of your intellect and emotions. Don't look for the quick and simplistic answers that seem to have worked for other people. Don't have that attitude: "Let me save you the trouble; learn from my mistakes." What an absurd statement that is. Think about it: How can you find the answers to your unique set of life issues by copying someone else's journey through their own unique issues? There are no shortcuts to learning life's deepest lessons. That mindset, while well-intentioned, minimizes your problem. It's like saying, "Your problem isn't any different from anyone else's . . . What worked for me will work for you." It's simply not true; you can't reduce your crisis to a formula. We don't grow or change or learn life's most vital lessons through mimicry. We learn through experience, through the pain (and yes, through the wonder) of embracing the journey.

What I hope you'll see is that if you own your questions and doubts and work toward your spiritual well-being from *within* your crisis, instead of looking past it, you will discover invaluable truth *in the midst of the journey* that you would not have found otherwise. Most of all—and I can't stress this point strongly enough—, don't let the fear of diminished faith stop you from engaging in the battle. Don't try to protect your faith by avoiding the battle. *Anything worth holding on to is worth fighting for.* Don't put a time limit on how long you're willing to fight this battle before you check out and go back to the nominal faith you formerly held just to avoid the uncomfortable process of working through it. If it's too easy for you to disengage from the battle, that's a sure indication that you weren't serious about fighting for your faith in the first place. As counterintuitive as it may seem, don't be afraid to allow your doubts to take you to places in your thoughts and emotions to which you would otherwise not be willing to go. I resonate deeply with Rachel Evans, who said, "My journey . . . like most journeys of faith, is a meandering and ongoing one, a story still in draft." I love her characterization of those who she calls "saints of holy curiosity whose lives of faithful questioning taught me not to fear my doubts, but to embrace and learn from them."[2] Like Evans, I have come to the place where I can no longer gloss over my own personal doubts and hope they will go away, nor do I desire to take that course of action. Doing so has not served me in the past. It is a wasteful, repetitive, and futile exercise.

And so, even now, on a crisp fall Sunday morning as I write about my faith, during that hour when I would normally be in attendance at church services, as I have always done until recently, I feel a certain awkwardness from not being in church, where my reflex and natural impulse would lead me. There's a sense of being off-balance for purposely stepping away from an established routine. But at the same time, my intuition is that it is a necessary and worthwhile stepping away for the purpose of looking at things from the outside, from the point of view of an impartial observer. Habits—even good ones, such as regular church attendance—can become futile when they're done purely out of a motivation to maintain a level of performance or consistency. And habits—even good ones—are hard to step away from, even when they grow stale. It's interesting that Albert Einstein, who, contrary to popular perception, had a deeply religious sensibility but had estranged himself from his religious community, said, "I have been absent from a synagogue so long that I'm afraid God would not recognize me."[3] For me as well, separating from my religious community, while liberating in one respect, also brings with it that feeling of estrangement—both from God and from my fellow observant Christians.

So, I've written this book, first of all, to show what an unresolved faith journey looks like. Why? Because I think there are others—perhaps many others—who are walking through their own unresolved faith journeys. If that's you, I want to encourage you to embrace that battle, no matter what the cost, because it's worth it. I've quoted Rachel Evans a few times already because she is so articulate on this point, but I completely understand what she meant when she wrote, "I didn't want to put my church story in print

---

2. Rachel Evans, *Inspired: Slaying Giants, Walking on Water, and Loving the Bible Again* (Nashville, TN: Nelson Books/HarperCollins, 2018), page xix.

3. Robert N. Goldman, *Einstein's God: Albert Einstein's Quest As a Scientist and as a Jew to Replace a Forsaken God* (Lanham, MD: Jason Aronson Inc., 1997), page 1.

because the truth is, I still don't know the ending."[4] It's true—as this book nears completion and the reality of publication looms large, it becomes clear that there *is* a cost to writing this book and putting my story out there, especially to those who know me best. But while I admit that I haven't exhaustively thought through the ramifications, it seems clear that the benefit of being open about my journey will justify the cost. Time will tell.

Reason Two: To Address Conflicting Images Of God

I've also written this book because my faith journey (or perhaps I should call it what it is: my faith crisis) is deeply rooted in my view of how Scripture reveals God's attitude toward his created beings—most specifically, those who the Bible seems to portray as outside of God's "chosen" community. My faith crisis is essentially because of that biblical idea, which is most frequently expressed by concepts like election, predestination, appointing, choosing, etc.

My thoughts here revolve around what I believe is an imbalanced or even unwarranted notion of how the character of God is portrayed by some of the more callous elements in the evangelical community. This point was driven home to me recently in dramatic fashion when I received an email from an observant Christian portraying God as a vindictive overlord who has actually brought on the coronavirus that plagues the entire world as I write—a God who has "taken away everything we worship." While thankfully not typical of most evangelical Christians, this offensive mindset does exist and does express itself from time to time when natural disaster strikes.

What I hope to show is that because of a selective reading or a misreading of the Bible, or by what surely seem to be false ideas about the character of God, and in some cases because of what I consider to be misguided notions by biblical authors, evangelical Christianity, while using language that characterizes God as loving, merciful, and just, also portrays another side of God's character—a completely opposite side, and I believe a false

---

4. Rachel Evans, *Searching for Sunday: Loving, Leaving, and Finding the Church* (Nashville, TN: Nelson Books/HarperCollins, 2015), page xv.

side—a God who, in some cases, is portrayed as unloving, unmerciful, vindictive, and unjust. That's a loaded statement! I fully realize that it might very well cause my evangelical readers to toss this book aside as sacrilege, unworthy to be taken seriously. But it's a statement from which I cannot back down. By raising the question of the reliability of biblical authorship, I realize that I'm questioning the sacred and cherished idea of biblical inspiration. But whether or not you agree with my viewpoint here, I urge you to read on. Don't be afraid to ask the questions that you consider off-limits—questions that might be lurking in the untapped corners of your mind but that you're hesitant to ask because they seem disrespectful or profane. I'm realizing that faith, if it is serious, must be characterized by a willingness to ask the hard questions and to live with some of those questions being unanswered for now without being fearful. I'm not asking you to concede that those questions won't ever be answered; that would be a defeatist and futile attitude. All I'm saying is that I urge you to take your questions and doubts seriously enough to deal with them honestly. My hope is that this book will encourage you to do that.

You might be asking at this point: What is the merit of faith if one is willing to give it up when the going gets rough? What about the Apostle Paul's injunction to "walk by faith, not by sight" (2 Corinthians 5:7) as we make our way through the trials of life? A natural and good question; solid biblical arguments can be made for doing just that. But let's not rush to that solution. It bypasses the valuable process of working through the questions and issues that brought you to the point in your journey where you now find yourself. For now, consider the following question: Assuming that faith can only be properly placed in one who proves to be a worthy object of that faith, what happens when that faith seems to produce no response? How does one sustain trust in the object of his or her faith when that object isn't responsive?

At the risk of appearing to be disloyal to my evangelical roots, it has become clear to me that, as Jon Sweeney put it, "Christianity holds what seem to be contradictory images of God almost simultaneously."[5] Sweeney cites two gospel texts to illustrate his point: the parable of Jesus as the Good Shepherd who cares deeply for even one lost sheep out of a flock of 100 (Luke 15:4) and the parable of the Great Banquet, in which Jesus is compared to a king who hosts a wedding feast for his son (Matthew 22). He invites strangers to the feast because his invited guests fail to attend. But when one of the guests shows up wearing the wrong clothing, the king says, "Bind him hand and foot, and throw him into the outer darkness; in that place there will be weeping and gnashing of teeth. For many are called, but few are chosen." We see here two completely different and irreconcilable images of God: one grace-filled, the other retributive and merciless. Both stories are parables, meaning that they are allegorical; their meaning goes beyond the plain text. But the second parable is, on the surface, a harrowing story, revealing a picture of God that seems very questionable, if not downright impossible. While I'm aware that evangelical Christians would deny (or justify) this punitive, retributive picture of God, I would argue that to be true to their adherence to biblical inerrancy, they can't avoid seeing this other portrayal of God's character—the punitive side— and proposing creative ways to mitigate it or explain it away. That harsh and punitive side of God's character is a necessary outgrowth of their view of God's attribute of justice.

Evangelicals typically resort to biblical texts such as Isaiah 55:8, "For my thoughts are not your thoughts, neither are your ways my ways," or 1 Corinthians 13:12, "We see through a glass, darkly," to back up their claim that God's ways are beyond our ability to discern, and therefore, we dare not question or judge God's "questionable actions," that they only seem to us to be incomprehensible because we can't possibly know the mind of God and therefore we're not qualified to judge his actions. I would argue, "Why not?" Indeed, the Bible itself encourages God's people to *know* him: for example, Jeremiah 31:34, "No longer will each man teach his neighbor or his brother, saying 'Know the Lord,' because they will *all* know me." Furthermore, to make "excuses" for the way God's actions are portrayed by

---

5. Jon M. Sweeney, *Inventing Hell: Dante, The Bible, and Eternal Torment* (Nashville, TN: Jericho Books, 2014), page 73.

the biblical authors—actions that are inexcusable by human standards—simply doesn't make sense in light of any reasonable definition of God as a merciful and loving God. Neither does it make sense in light of the Christian belief in the fallen nature of man; for even in his fallen state, man is still created in God's image. God's "image-bearer" therefore retains the goodness of God's image in his character, even if to a diminished degree. So any departure from that God-image is anomaly, not the natural disposition of human nature. That is why the creation/fall story in Genesis takes us by shock—a perfect paradise story so quickly turned bad!

The evangelical claim that humanity completely lost its God-image in the fall, so there is no longer any good in man and therefore nothing man does can be redeemable as good, is absurd simply through observation of the goodness displayed by humanity. So we must face the all-important question of how to understand the blatantly obvious disconnection between the Bible's portrayal of God as being both merciful and punishing, both knowable and unknowable. Again, I realize that it is our natural inclination, out of veneration for God's greatness, to point to all kinds of reasonable justifications in defense of God's character that immediately come to mind, but I urge you to be patient, read on, and journey with me as we explore and seek to understand what certainly seem to be mystifying aspects of the character of God as portrayed in Scripture.

To summarize, those are the two reasons for this book: (1) to describe an evolving faith journey, that is, a journey still in progress and not resolved, (2) *because of* the conflicting biblical portrayals of God, the object of that faith.

* * *

I'll present my central argument in Part Three, where I discuss what I would best describe as a disparaging and false view of God as portrayed not only by evangelical Christianity, but also by the Apostle Paul himself: a God whose character is misrepresented by the commonly held orthodox Christian view that portrays him in two entirely opposite ways: as loving, merciful, and gracious, but also as a God who exhibits the opposites of those characteristics. My claim is that this other, negative and vindictive portrayal of God is unwarranted and unjustifiable, based on a universally accepted understanding what the nature of a "good" god must be. My central argument will be to show how the apostle Paul misinterpreted Old Testament texts, completely changing the clear meaning and message of those texts.

PART ONE

Setting Out on a Faith Journey

The Courage to Be is rooted in the God who appears
When God has disappeared in the anxiety of doubt.

—Paul Tillich, *The Courage to Be*

Many people are perplexed, even troubled, by the fact that God (if such
there be) has not made His existence sufficiently clear.

—Daniel Howard-Snyder & Paul K. Moser, *Divine Hiddenness*

The Risk, Power, And Mystery Of Faith

Perhaps the reason it's so difficult to talk about faith is because it is so multifaceted as a phenomenon. That it is a risk is self-evident—there are obvious potential consequences (whether good or harmful) depending on whether you embrace it or not. It's also powerful—it can alter the course of one's life for the good, or it can destroy one's confidence if it is unreciprocated. And finally, faith is certainly a mystery; even to embrace it is not necessarily to fully understand it or to be fully convinced of its merit. Let's start out on the journey by looking at these three elements of faith: its risk, its power, and its mystery.

The risk of a faith journey

By its nature, faith is never static. It is either strong or weak, and it varies in its strength or weakness depending on how it is influenced by forces outside of it. Sometimes those influences are almost imperceptible, for example, when a repeated behavior brings about a predictable outcome, resulting in a pattern of expectation. But at other times those influences are noticeable and definitive, such as when a specific prayer for the seemingly impossible healing of a loved one is miraculously and tangibly answered, leaving little or no doubt that the prayer was instrumental in bringing about the result.

Another characteristic of faith is that we know intuitively what should and should not be a reasonable or worthy object of our faith. This intuition comes from the experience of having placed one's faith in someone or something that has proven to either reward or disappoint. Those are instances of the exercise or nonexercise of faith.

But a *faith journey* is much more. Beyond those occasions where we exercise single acts of faith, as people of faith, we all embark at some point on a faith journey, whether early or later in life, whether once or frequently. But we don't all experience a faith crisis—that is, a crisis brought about by the seeming failure of one's wavering faith to be restored. There is risk involved in faith. Sometimes we say our faith is "shaken." (Interestingly, there's even a "Shaken Faith" legal doctrine that describes the confidence or lack of confidence or peace of mind that the buyer of a new car feels. The doctrine states that "once the buyer's faith is shaken, the vehicle loses not only its real value in their eyes but becomes an instrument whose integrity is substantially impaired and whose operation is fraught with apprehension.") The illustration is incomplete, but it does demonstrate the point that faith *is* an investment of oneself based on the proposed reliability of the "product" that one receives in return for the investment—in the context of this book, that product is the confidence of God's favor. In some ways, like investing in a new car or a house, investing in faith is a risk.

But back to my point: Struggles of faith vary in their intensity. Faith crises don't come out of nowhere. There's always a reason, whether it be a tragedy, failure, disappointment, disillusionment, etc. For me, that reason is quite simple. *I'm seeking a reasonable explanation about the universally understood character of a good God in the context of a scriptural tradition that can be confusing at best and inflammatory in its portrayal of God at worst.* After a lifetime of observance and practice as a believer, I simply have not been able to reconcile the idea of a "Good God"—and all that encompasses in our understanding and imagination—with how the Bible, to a great extent, portrays that God. Let me say up front (and this is a vital point, on which I'll expand later) that as one who believes in God, I cannot believe that God can be anything but good. So, it can only follow that I'm inclined to reject any "evidence" that would portray him to the contrary.

While there are workable and even rational explanations for Scripture's seemingly confused portrayal of God's character, a completely satisfying solution does not present itself unambiguously. An explanation merely seeks to accept a proposition, despite the incongruity, whereas a solution satisfies or resolves the incongruity. As a lifelong student of the Bible in both evangelical and secular educational environments, I've been searching long and hard for a solution to the problem of the ambiguity of the Biblical image of God, as those people with whom I've shared my views can confirm. It seems clear that for those who regard the biblical text as sacred, the best we can strive for, and in fact our only recourse with regard to questions about God's character, is to formulate an explanation based on an honest reading of the biblical record, which is, after all, the authoritative biography (or, as a strict biblical literalist would put it, the autobiography) of God, regardless of whether or not such an explanation brings about intellectual satisfaction. And that is, in fact, exactly what we're doing when we defend God's character. Our positive judgment of God's character as "good" is based on what we recognize and accept as the authoritative text on the subject of God: the Bible. And while we are careful to back up our assessment of his goodness with particular evidences of that goodness, in the end, we claim that the authoritative text about his character as "good" must be the standard, regardless of our particular experiences of that quality. We are conditioned to agree with what we see as the Bible's overarching portrayal of a good God despite portions of that same text that portray what seems to be an opposite side. It is a sort of unwritten rule that, as evangelicals, we simply don't question or challenge what appear to be conflicting (or even false) representations in the biblical text itself of a good and loving God.

That's why I say it's so important to own your unique spiritual journey. Don't look for quick and easy answers here; you won't find any. Be okay with the questions, even the ones that linger unresolved, seemingly without end (remember Evans' "life of holy questioning"), because those are the kinds of questions that will keep you engaged in your quest for truth. My hope is that you will gain from my story some recognition as to where you are in your own spiritual journey, and perhaps, you'll be motivated to dig deeper and come closer to finding your way through your crisis, or at least an explanation that you can work with. The most important thing is to keep seeking. In Paul Tillich's book *The New Being*, he writes in a chapter appropriately titled "What is Truth": "He who asks seriously the questions of the truth that liberates is already on his way to liberation . . . He may still be in the bondage of cynical despair, but he has already started to emerge from it."[6]

As you read on, you will no doubt notice what will seem to be not-so-subtle conflicting viewpoints here and there throughout this book. At some points it will seem that I am contradicting what I wrote earlier, or that I have changed my mind about certain convictions. I hope you will under-

---

6. Paul Tillich, *The New Being* (New York: Charles Scribner's Sons, 1955), page 72.

stand that this is in the spirit of the candid and honest dialogue that's on-going in my own life, even as I write, and that is, in fact, why I have written this book. As I hinted above, my journey is far from over. So rather than attempting to present a harmonized account that leads to resolution, I have intentionally written out of a place of unsettledness in my convictions, so there will naturally be conflicting views that emerge from my own thought process. This is to be expected if I am to represent my journey honestly. You might be inclined to judge that conflict as "confusion" on my part. That's okay; it's a risk I take in revealing my journey with such honesty and in such depth. In fact, navigating through the issues that arise in this quest can be quite confusing at times. I would just urge you to keep in mind that my purpose is not simply to try to resolve the obvious conflicting viewpoints. Rather, recognize that just as it is sometimes difficult to harmonize one's biblical and theological positions, so it is equally hard to harmonize one's own fluctuating views of that body of belief. This is true even for those who were closest to Jesus as he moved and acted in real everyday encounters, as the two following stories illustrate.

The power of faith and the power of doubt

There are two narratives about Jesus in the Gospel of Mark that are in stark contrast with each other, but that stand out to illustrate my personal journey of faith—a story of strong and unwavering faith and a story of utter skepticism. In Mark chapter 5, Jesus heals a woman who has a blood disease. She is described as a woman of great faith: "If I touch even his garments, I will be made well," and in fact, that's exactly what happens. She pushes her way through a crowd to get to Jesus and touches his clothing, and "immediately the flow of blood dried up, and she felt in her body that she was healed of her disease." When Jesus asks, "Who touched my garments?" She approaches timidly ("in fear and trembling") and owns up to being the guilty party. Jesus responds: "Daughter, *your faith has made you well*; go in peace and be healed of your disease."

In the second story (Mark chapter 6), we find Jesus in his hometown of Nazareth, where he's teaching in a synagogue. The people listen in aston-ishment, not knowing what to make of his wisdom and power to heal, since, after all, he was just an ordinary citizen of Nazareth, a carpenter, whose unassuming family background they knew well. As Mark tells us, "They took offense at him," and Mark draws our attention to the startling reality that Jesus "could do no mighty work there, except that he laid his hands on a few sick people and healed them."

In the first story, the woman's faith is not only effective to believe that Jesus has the ability to heal, but it is *her faith itself* that healed her. The power of her faith was such that it is described by Jesus as the effective cause or source of the healing power. We are startled by the seemingly impassive attitude of Jesus as he doesn't even seem to realize what was happening, only that power had gone out from him. The story is odd—it is told in a way that portrays Jesus as the obvious source of power behind the miracle, and yet at the same time an inactive participant in it.

But the second account is even more startling. We have here another story about the effect of power, only now it is the power of unbelief—the unbelief of those who couldn't reconcile the miracles they were witnessing with their preconceived ideas of who Jesus was: an ordinary man living among them (at least up until now), in ordinary community. They refused to accept the obvious implications of what they were seeing with their own eyes and what God himself declared openly in Mark 1:11—that Jesus was the son of God. Their unbelief was actually effective in *limiting* the ability of the son of God to do "mighty works."

In the first story, faith *activates* Jesus' power; in the second story, the lack of faith actually *negates* Jesus's power.

These stories serve to bring to light some questions that I grapple with in my own personal journey of faith. Did Jesus literally mean what he said: "*Your* faith has made you well"? Is it possible for one's faith—for my faith—to be strong enough, to be effective enough, to produce life-changing results? And, conversely, can my lack of faith—my persistent questions and doubts, even my unbelief—be powerful enough to effectively prohibit God's ability to act, to "do mighty works?" These questions point back to an even more foundational question, a question that I think everyone must wrestle with at one time or another, regardless of whether or not they would dare to admit it—is faith real? Or is it, as Freud described it in *The Future of an Illusion*, "a system of wishful illusions together with a disavowal of reality, such as we find nowhere else but in a state of blissful . . . confusion"? Richard Holloway was more decisive when he wrote:

> Objective certainty is not available to us in this life. There is of course subjective conviction, but that is a private thing which, of itself, proves nothing. Since we cannot, in the nature of the case, know for certain on this side of death what lies on the other side, *there is really no way of absolutely demonstrating either the delusional nature of religion or its reality.*[7] (italics added)

That last line of Paul Tillich's book *The Courage to Be* (quoted at the head of this chapter) speaks to me in a powerful way. It says to me that periods of spiritual doubt in the life of a believer are not only unavoidable, but they have the potential, if treated honestly, to alter the development of one's view of God and spirituality in a life-transforming way. The key is honesty with yourself and the courage to accept and embrace the discomfort of not knowing the most vital truth about yourself: what you believe to be objective truth—that is, truth held without bias caused by feelings, ideas, opinions, etc. Tillich explains what he means by the "courage to be." He calls it the "fundamental existential question . . . Is there an alternative to chaos and despair? If so, how does one, with the will to believe, find it?"[8] Peter Berger comments on what he sees as a shallow and shortsighted (but, unfortunately, typical) treatment of doubt: "Doubts are dispelled by being given a negative status. In religious cases, they are subsumed under the heading of sin; thus a lack of faith is deemed sinful, a rebellion against God."[9]

---

7. Richard Holloway: *Crossfire: Faith and Doubt in an Age of Uncertainty* (Grand Rapids, MI: Eerdmans Publishing, 1988), page 35.

8. Paul Tillich, *The Courage to Be* (New Haven, CT: Yale University Press, 1980), page xix.

9. Peter Berger, *In Praise of Doubt: How to Have Convictions without Becoming a Fanatic* (New York: HarperCollins, 2009), page 85.

Berger goes on to reflect on the positive value of doubt, which is not typically viewed as such by most people. For me, it is becoming both a safe place and a worthwhile journey. In a recent sermon on Luke chapter 7 titled "Doubters Welcome, Jeffrey Boettcher made the point that doubt is not an absence of faith but actually can lead to a more robust and well thought-out faith *if the doubts are honest.* The condition in that statement shouldn't be missed. Doubt *can* lead to a stronger faith. But it's not a given. The negative side of that claim is obviously that honest doubts *can* also lead to a weaker or compromised faith. I appreciate the nonsimplistic nature of that subtlety. As Richard Holloway wrote, "Dishonest belief is a greater danger to faith than honest disbelief."[10] As Boettcher noted in that sermon, it is important to judge our own doubts—whether they are honest or dishonest. Honest doubt is doubt that seeks answers and has as its goal the discovery of truth, while dishonest doubt digs in and seeks to establish itself as justified and therefore does not seek resolution. The temptation is to become indifferent, to "dig in," to simply concede the battle. At times, the battle becomes so tiresome that it seems to be a battle even to decide whether or not to go on with the battle.

In writing about his own faith journey, Richard Rohr talks about doubt as a conflict between head and heart:

> We all came into this world gifted with innocence, but gradually, as we became more intelligent, we lost our innocence. We were born with silence, and as we grew up, we lost the silence and were filled with words. We lived in our hearts, and as time passed, we moved into our heads. Now the reversal of this journey is enlightenment. It is the journey from head back to the heart, from words, back to silence; *getting back to our innocence in spite of our intelligence.*[11] (italics added)

We are constantly fighting an internal battle between head and heart. As thinking and feeling creatures, we are so often torn between the two con-

---

10. Richard Holloway, *Dancing on the Edge: Faith in a Post-Christian Age* (New York: HarperCollins, 1997), page 14.

11. Richard Rohr, "My Own Journey," https://cac.org/my-own-journey-2019-03-25/

flicting influences of intellect and emotions. As Rohr wisely points out, it is the element of enlightenment that motivates us, or gives us the ability, to live our lives in the most rewarding and productive way. The wisdom gained·through the course of a lifetime is a precious resource that, if nurtured wisely, can guide us to a place where we will intuitively live with a better awareness and ability to navigate life's uncertainties.

In his book *The Future of Faith*, Harvey Cox writes that "to call oneself a practicing Christian, but not necessarily a believing one, acknowledges the variable admixture of certainties and uncertainties that mark the life of any religious person."[12] Having been a practicing Christian for most of my life, I have lived through periods of unbelief and restored belief at different stages. I have battled from time to time, as most if not all believers do, with periods of doubt. Cox points out that even Mother Teresa "confessed that for years she had harbored troubling doubt about the existence of God, even as she worked ceaselessly to relieve the anguish of the sick and dying in Calcutta."[13] So my experience is not untypical of others who have struggled with doubt (indeed, some, like Mother Teresa, whose lives have exhibited an extreme measure of faith).

The usual way most people navigate through doubt is to involve themselves in an affirming spiritual environment in which doubt is diminished by surrounding positive influences, drawing the doubter back from his waywardness. That's why, for example, churches stress the importance of small groups, or "community groups," where a more intimate setting provides an atmosphere where people can encourage one another in their spiritual walk. By their nature, small groups that are geared toward openness on the part of participants are effective only when two conditions characterize the group: (1) members of the group are open about their spiritual condition, open about their doubts, and (2) there is a "safe" environment, meaning the absence of judgment or even corrective feedback. Once trust is compromised (either judgmentally or through well-intentioned criticism), participants no longer feel safe in such environments, and group participation

---

12. Harvey Cox, *The Future of Faith* (New York: HarperCollins, 2009), page 17.
13. Ibid, page 17.

becomes shallow and superficial, and thus incapable of effectively helping the doubter/questioner.

Having led small groups, it has been my experience that when group participation becomes perfunctory due to a breakdown of trust, it loses its dynamic as a worthwhile practice; people put up their defenses and shut down; and the meeting evolves into a social gathering or a superficial question/answer session, with little if any depth of spiritual engagement. It takes on a sort of assertive "catechismal" tone, devolving from real encounter with meaningful dialog (with or without resolution) to a situation where the most "correct" and simplistic "biblical" answer (no matter how superficial) is sought out and, once found, is agreed upon and settles the question for the participants. I have led small groups where well-meaning participants have shut down and "checked out" midmeeting due to an unthoughtful challenge or insensitive comment from another member of the group.

To elaborate a bit more on this peculiar phenomenon so often characteristic of Christian small group meetings, it often happens that agreement on "biblical correctness" takes such a prominent place that it seems to leave no space for creative, stimulating, and even argumentative and challenging discussion. There's an intrinsic fear of going off-course from the conventional denominational line on which participants are expected to agree. In one respect I get it. We as Christians are most comfortable in group settings when our theology is well defined; we tend to sense danger and lose our heads when quick and easy biblical answers don't immediately present themselves. We are conditioned in the evangelical environment to seek out "correct doctrine" above all other encounters with the biblical text. We become so conditioned, in fact, that we are in a place of spiritual discomfort when we are unsure of a faith tenet that our church espouses as the correct interpretive standard on which we are expected to take a rigid stand, or with which we are assumed to be in conformity. Whether or not we discern a check in our intellect with regard to that declared or standard interpretation, we (in the evangelical community) are most comfortable when we have "settled" on the matter, regardless of whether or not it genuinely rings true to our intellect.

My point is that clearly there is a deeper level of doubt that occurs in the lives of some believers—one that might be most popularly described as the "dark night of the soul," or what Viktor Frankl calls the "existential vacuum," or more specifically, what Paul Tillich (in *The Courage to Be*) calls the "anxiety of meaninglessness and doubt." Tillich asks a compelling question, the question that might well summarize everything I'm trying to say in this book: "Is there a kind of faith which can exist together with doubt and meaninglessness?"[14]

In his Introduction to Tillich's book, Peter Gomes simplifies and sums up Tillich's thesis about believing *in spite of* what you see:

> Genuine belief is maintained in spite of circumstances that would undermine belief and not simply because of circumstances that would confirm it. It does not take a great deal of imagination or courage to believe that God is on your side when you are prospering or winning; it takes a great deal of courage and imagination to believe that God is on your side when you are suffering or losing . . .[15]

It requires an inordinate amount of courage and resolve to maintain genuine faith when you don't see any evidence of that faith leading to the spiritual wellbeing that you're looking for or that you've been conditioned to expect all your life. When you experience little or no tangible response from God, does it not take a tremendous act of your will to keep on believing that God is real, that he is good, and that he cares about you? As Rudolf Otto said, "It is one thing merely to believe in a reality beyond the senses and another to have experience of it also; it is one thing to have ideas of the holy, and another to become consciously aware of it as an operative reality."[16]

---

14. Paul Tillich, *The Courage to Be* (New Haven, CT: Yale University Press, 1980), page 174.

15. Ibid, page xxiii.

16. Rudolf Otto, *The Idea of the Holy* (New York: Oxford University Press, 1958), page 143.

A typical Evangelical counterargument to the idea of God's nonresponsive-
ness would go something like this: God *has* responded by revealing himself
in his son Jesus, who is God in flesh, who lived, died, and was resurrected
as irrefutable proof that he is real, that he is good, and that he cares about
you. After all, what greater proof could there be of his goodness than his
claim to be the savior of the world and validation of that claim by his resurrection from death? To evangelicals, the empty tomb is irrefutable evidence
that settles any doubt about the reality of God and his active involvement
in human affairs. - why?

That argument is solid and difficult to refute from a purely theological perspective, but it fails to answer the gut-level question above: How is one to
believe in God's active presence when there is no tangible evidence? C. S.
Lewis talks about the relationship between belief and evidence:

> There are some who moderately opine that there is, or is not, a
> God. But there are others whose belief or disbelief is free from
> doubt. And all these beliefs, weak or strong, are based on what
> appears to the holders to be evidence; but the strong believers or
> disbelievers of course think they have a very strong evidence.[17]

One could argue that when a decision is made to believe in and follow
God, one must be prepared to accept or endure a degree of elusiveness in
the mystery. One must be able to be comfortable with waiting because we
can't pursue revelation; rather, revelation *comes to us.* But when (after 60-
plus years) you experience little or no *tangible* response from God, how
does the adherence to a theological dogma sustain you?

In our Christian circles, we are usually conditioned to the idea that, when
there's a distance between me and God, it's never God's fault because God
is always pursuing us, and we're not doing our part in reaching back in
response to God. But isn't it true (in general) when we're dealing with
emotional or physical struggles or experiencing personal doubt, that our

---

17. C. S. Lewis, "On Obstinacy in Belief" in *The World's Last Night* (New York: Harcourt Brace &
Co., 1987), page 21.

first instinct is to blame God for keeping a distance, for being silent, or even for being angry with us? Our temptation is to justify our doubt as the only reasonable response to forces outside our control that seem to make that doubt justifiable, and that entertaining doubt is therefore a logical response, and therefore to walk through it and talk about it in a way that rationalizes that doubt.

Why does such a response seem to make the most sense? Because the alternative (indeed, the typical Evangelical response) is to embrace the possibility that my diagnosis of the problem was all wrong—that after all it isn't God who is being silent, it isn't God who is withholding a revelation of His truth and goodness to me. It is rather that I have drawn the wrong conclusion about God's seeming distance, that He really isn't withholding His presence; that He's present in what is often called His "still small voice" (like the voice the prophet Elijah heard and responded to, in 1 Kings 9:11–13:   *really!.*

> The Lord passed by, and a great and strong wind tore into the mountains and broke the rocks in pieces before the Lord, *but the Lord was not in the wind*; and after the wind, an earthquake, *but the Lord was not in the earthquake*; and after the earthquake a fire, *but the Lord was not in the fire*; and after the fire, a *still small voice.* [the voice that Elijah actually heard and responded to!]

But let's be real—for all but the most spiritually receptive among us, that "voice," if it's even out there, is so still and so small as to be imperceptible. So our conditioned response to God's seeming silence is to turn inward and draw the conclusion that "Perhaps, I'm just not listening; I've wandered away from God's presence without justifiable cause." That would put me in the position of having to take the first step toward God, regardless of whether or not He chooses to reciprocate, putting me at risk of being ignored by God despite my best efforts, and it would put me right back into the cycle of questioning whether God is real. So the questions and doubts would persist, and I would be back to square one.

The very obvious and practical basis for this kind of reasoning is simply the notion that communication and relationship, to be effective, must be a two-way street. Rather, my instinct is to go where the doubt leads me, to be brave and honest enough to allow it to play out in its natural course, accepting the "dark side" of what that choice very well might mean—further estrangement from the faith that was once unquestioned. Peter Berger summarizes the double-sided problem of doubt when he writes:

> If not a fanatic true believer like Calvin, the believer lives with and in faith that is troubled by doubt. If not a fanatic atheist like [a] Darwinist, the agnostic lives with and in doubt that is troubled by faith. It's a thin line, but an essential divide.[18]

I would agree that there's a thin line between the two. To have "faith that is troubled by doubt" is not that far removed from the alternative (doubt troubled by faith). Neither condition is hopeless. As Holloway writes, those who are "troubled by the possibility of faith feel themselves to be on the very edge of it, yet their very honesty keeps them from moving more confidently into the community of believers. Far from being an act of courage, such a gesture would, for them, be a surrender of personal integrity."[19] As I hope to show, a weak faith, a faith troubled by doubt, is a condition that most of us (at least those of us who are not troubled with the stoicism of Calvinism) face from time to time, a condition that, if taken seriously and not pushed aside as inconvenient and bothersome, can potentially ignite a spark of hope for spiritual renewal.

The Bible often portrays God as complicated and dynamic in his relations with man. The Jewish patriarchs, including Abraham, Jacob, and Joseph come to mind. As Rachel Evans puts it: "Our most sacred stories emerged from a rift in that relationship, an intense crisis of faith. Those of us who

---

18. Peter Berger, *In Praise of Doubt: How to Have Convictions without Becoming a Fanatic* (New York: HarperCollins, 2009), page 109.

19. Richard Holloway, *Dancing on the Edge: Faith in a Post-Christian Age.* (New York: HarperCollins, 1997), page 23.

spend as much time doubting as we do believing can take enormous comfort in that."[20]

I've often thought of Blaise Pascal's famous characterization of faith as a wager. Simply put, what do you have to lose by believing? He says that, as rational beings, we should live life as though God exists. If God doesn't exist, you've lost nothing but some of the pleasures of living a self-centered life. But if God does exist, and you rejected Him, you've lost everything for all of eternity.[21] That simple reasoning immediately makes sense on the surface. Pascal's wager—to live life in view of future reward or punishment (a blissful afterlife or a hellish eternal existence) is a difficult proposition to argue against. If there is life after death, we instinctually wish to live in a way that will guarantee that bliss to come. But it's easier said than done. Can I "choose" to believe just because the promised reward of belief is more appealing (in light of the possibility of eternal life) than unbelief? Or is it more realistic, not to mention more honest, to embrace Richard Kearney's idea that ". . . the oscillation between doubt and faith as a choice to be made over and over, never once and for all?"[22]

Contentment with the mystery

I find it awkward to write about my own spiritual journey. I struggle to be completely open about my journey because, as I think it is becoming clear and will become even clearer, at many points it is fraught with doubt, skepticism, and unresolved questions. And I am aware of the risk involved. In fact, some of those closest to me have encouraged me not to put this book out there because it could potentially be a weakening or damaging influence to other believing Christians in my evangelical circle. While I don't take such warnings lightly, at the same time my sense is that it is important enough to talk about openly, since my purpose is to describe my

---

20. Rachel Evans, *Inspired: Slaying Giants, Walking on Water, and Loving the Bible Again* (Nashville, TN: Nelson Books/HarperCollins, 2018), page 14.

21. For Pascal's full explanation of the Wager, see *Pascal Pensees*, translated by A. J. Krailsheimer. (New York: Penguin Books, 1966), pages 149–154.

22. Richard Kearney, *Anatheism: Returning to God after God* (New York: Columbia University Press, 2011), page 56.

journey honestly and genuinely because, again, surely I'm not alone among my fellow believers in fighting this battle.

Since I've lived virtually my entire life as a believing Christian, it isn't easy to expose some of my deepest doubts and questions with regard to religious, biblical, and spiritual matters. We all live some areas of our lives behind a façade that we work hard to represent as the way we want people to see us. It's built into our nature to project an image of our own design, an image that represents us in the light of our most positive self-image. We are most secure when we hold firmly to certain beliefs and when we are confident in our convictions. When that certainty begins to crumble, when we decide to be completely honest about our belief system or come to the place where we are unsettled about what we believe, at the deepest core of our being—no matter where it takes us—, it brings us into a place of vulnerability, open to judgment, exposed for who we truly are, not the image we have so carefully crafted about ourselves. Simply put, we all have areas of baggage in our thought lives that we'd rather not unpack, whether they be spiritual, emotional, or whatever. But there's another side, an opposite side, of uncertainty, which is positive—what Gregory Boyd called the "Benefit of the Doubt"[23] and is summarized by Richard Holloway:

> Living in the crossfire between the compulsion of opposing certainties will always be demanding, but it will not infrequently be exhilarating. Those who live out there . . . may be far out in no-man's land, away from the big guns with their booming certainties, but they do learn to survive . . . Faith has its conflicts, but it also has its mysterious consolations.[24]

I'm discovering, even as I write, that it's both liberating and healing to tell the truth about my spiritual condition, even if surprising (and perhaps in some cases, shocking) to those who know me best. I've wrestled long and hard with much of what I write in this book, and while there is incremental

---

23. Gregory A. Boyd, *Benefit of the Doubt: Breaking the Idol of Certainty* (Grand Rapids, MI: Baker Books, 2013).

24. Richard Holloway, *Crossfire: Faith and Doubt in an Age of Uncertainty* (Grand Rapids, MI: Eerdmans Publishing, 1988), page 154.

and satisfying resolution from time to time, I continue to wrestle with the ideas I've presented here. As Holloway summarizes it in the excerpt above, my faith has conflicts, as well as "mysterious consolations." But I've come to the conclusion that it does no good to internalize our most troublesome inner struggles to the point where we come to believe that they are unique to us, that no one would understand. As I hinted above, I believe that we all have deep-seated internal struggles that we wrestle with. Most of the time (as has been true for me), we're content to go inward and work through them on our own so as not to trouble the people in our lives who care about us. But sometimes we face an internal battle that seems so arduous, so tiresome, that we can no longer contain it within ourselves. That's why I wrote this book.

My biggest apprehension has been that it has always been important to me to exhibit resolve in spiritual matters for those closest to me by communicating certainty and conviction in my beliefs. In my role as a spouse, father, friend, coworker, and (at times) church leader, it has always weighed on me to be someone who is there for the people in my life through their own spiritual struggles. Until recent years, little did I expect that I would experience confidence in my core religious convictions eroding to the point where I would be challenging the very foundations of my own faith.

Taking a step backward

At different stages, I think we all (at least those of us who have held to a living faith tradition) find ourselves in a place where it seems wise to slow down and evaluate where we are in terms of our spiritual journey. Sometimes small adjustments (let's call them "renewals" or "revivals") are sufficient to put us back on track in our thinking. But sometimes our self-evaluation can become troublesome enough to elicit the urge to take a big step backward, to resist the temptation to rush through the spiritual crisis without addressing the underlying issues and to face what can look like an overwhelming obstacle to our faith; to accept the emotional distress of not knowing where we are; and to simply make a decision to deal with it at a depth that we haven't yet been willing to go, no matter what the level of anxiety or fear and no matter where it takes us. This is where I find myself to be.

For several years now, I've been sensing the need to consider seriously the trajectory of my faith journey. I'm recognizing the need to talk about what I have come to see as the most important area of struggle for me: my faith. I must grapple openly with the issues involving my faith that not only need to become more clear to me, or at least find articulate expression (if only to myself), but also perhaps (hopefully) to be of some benefit to others. Clarity of conviction is a gift to be cherished. Many of the Christians whose paths I've crossed have exhibited such confidence and assurance, and it is to be admired. But for me, complete clarity on issues regarding my faith is not something that has ever come easily for me, and even less so in recent years, for reasons that I hope you will see as you read on.

I often find myself thinking (and probably mostly overthinking) about life's "hard" questions—the kinds of questions that, instead of yielding answers, end up raising more questions. Perhaps I tend to dwell on those questions because I'm stubborn—I refuse to yield to the possibility that there might not be answers, that those questions might have to remain questions, mysteries of life that I just have to be satisfied to accept as unanswered, or even unanswerable, and go on with life. More and more I am of the opinion that this is *exactly* the case, that there are indeed questions—even questions about my own faith tradition—that must remain unanswered, and even unanswerable. Or perhaps there's a part of me that avoids reaching conclusions for fear that the answers are just too alarming.

It is a healthy and useful exercise to look back thoughtfully and critically on one's life, reflecting on the past after having called back to memory, thought through, assessed, reassessed, and drawn thoughtful conclusions about life lived so far. Also, because we each have our own unique spiritual journey and because we're each on a different path, we can learn important things when we look beyond our own journey and observe the lives of others as mirrors in some ways into our own lives. Sometimes the reflection you see in other people reveals things about you that are at odds with the way you've always seen yourself. But the mirror always tells the truth about you.

And while it's sometimes painful, knowing and dealing with the truth about oneself is the only way good and lasting change will happen. It's counterproductive (not to mention dishonest) to ignore what you see and go on telling yourself that everything is the same as it has always been. I want to be honest about my struggles in regard to my faith journey. And maybe you will see some of yourself in part of my story and be prompted to examine your own journey. At least that's my hope.

On the edge of Christianity

I have lived my whole life in an Evangelical Christian setting. I think my particular spiritual journey is in many ways much the same as those of many other Christians who have grown up in Evangelical environments similar to my own. But I also think that because of the direction my life has taken, especially my academic experience, which resulted in some particularly difficult intellectual struggles I have fought through (struggles that have only intensified as the years have progressed), I can perhaps offer some insights into struggles that some evangelical Christians have had to face. I do believe that there are others like me, who might be best described (in the words of Richard Holloway) as being "on the edge of Christianity"— evangelicals who grapple with some of the fundamental ideas and theological positions that characterize us as a group.

In large part, my struggle revolves around the idea that I have embraced certain basic evangelical ideas simply because, like them or not, they are the standard creed of Evangelicalism. To be more specific, some of those basic theological positions have simply ceased to be authentically biblical, to my thinking. As Holloway wrote: "It can never be right to expect anyone to submit to a form of words or a propositional encapsulation of the truth which they cannot accept without dishonesty and the violation of their own intellectual integrity."[25] Or as Brian McLaren put it more concisely, "the search for faith cannot bypass the intellect."[26] So I hope my experience

---

25. Richard Holloway, *Dancing on the Edge: Faith in a Post-Christian Age* (New York: HarperCollins, 1997), page xi.

26. Brian McLaren, *Finding Faith: A Self-Discovery Guide for Your Spiritual Quest* (Grand Rapids, MI: Zondervan Publishing, 1999), page 13.

will connect with some of you, and I have little doubt that I will certainly not connect with others. But whether my story resonates with you or not, since each of us does have a different, unique life story, the particular nuances of our life experiences can always be illuminating to others, even if in some small way. And perhaps my particular story will be of some help.

Some Questions About A Faith Journey

Big questions

If you live long enough and are honest enough (and perhaps brave enough) to think hard about life and grapple with the inevitable questions that arise in your mind over the course of time, you will almost certainly come to a place where you experience a confluence of spiritual, intellectual, and emotional questions or crises—perhaps more than once, but certainly I believe at least once. I mean the really big questions: What's my purpose in life? What lasting value will my life have to those I leave behind? And perhaps the most important question of all: *What do I believe to be the absolute truth?* Even using the term "absolute truth" shows that we somehow think there's a truth beyond what we might, at one time or another, consider to be truth—a more absolutely truthful truth than just the plain truth. As if the truth were "fairly true," but not quite true enough to qualify as "absolutely true."

But I think it's a useful distinction—many things about us are innately or intuitively true, and therefore undeniably true. I know that I am a living, thinking, and feeling creature (in Descartes's famous formulation of a statement that could not be doubted, "I think, therefore I am."). Some things are true about us, even if they aren't necessarily proven by observation (thus we can easily deceive others into seeing us other than as we truly are). But certainly there must be one absolute or definitive truth about all of us that dwarfs all other truths—the truth about our ultimate existence. The question, "Are we eternal beings?" is so foundational that I have little doubt that, if I were to ask you to be completely honest, you would agree that it is the question of ultimate concern. What, if anything, lies beyond this life for us? Or, to consider it as a consequential question: Does the faith

live a good life (following Christ) w/act
PART ONE: Setting Out on a Faith Journey *the reward*
of heaven
37

that I exhibit through my lifetime ultimately matter?" Does what I believe in this life with regard to the mysteries of God carry with it rewards or consequences in a life to come? Are there, or are there not, damning consequences for unbelief? The irony is that while these are certainly the most important questions anyone can ask, obviously no one (literally, *no one*) has ever answered them definitively. As Richard Holloway put it: ". . . there can be no leading or absolute proof on one side or the other: we cannot absolutely determine the rational certainty of the presence of something beyond ourselves . . . We are left therefore, with a calculated probability on the basis of which we act, and that action is called Faith."[27]

For those (very few I think) who are fortunate enough (or perhaps not so fortunate) to go blissfully through life without facing such existential questions, I'm afraid I don't have much to offer. As Thomas Dubay put it so candidly: "If you are untouched by a pervading agnosticism, you are rare."[28] Maybe some people simply reject, or suppress, the impulse to grapple with questions about what lies beyond. Or perhaps for some people, life just gets too busy, so that (again, fortunately or unfortunately) it never occurs to you to think beyond your next crisis, or your next career advancement, or whatever it is that drives some people to simply get along, survive, move on with life untroubled by such concerns. Or maybe you have managed to convince yourself that this is it; it's not even a question; there's nothing else beyond this life, so why bother thinking about it? Although my sense is that it would be unlikely to find anyone who would claim to be completely unmoved by the big questions I'm talking about.

But to be a little more generous of human nature, most people regard it as a life well lived in which they strive to learn, succeed, grow, and indeed use wisely in every way the lifetime that they have been given. Most of us want to live life with a sense of wanting to take it seriously, work hard, and achieve something truly valuable that we can leave behind. Furthermore, I would suggest that no serious person (no matter how well they live life,

---

27. Richard Holloway: *Crossfire: Faith and Doubt in an Age of Uncertainty* (Grand Rapids, MI: Eerdmans Publishing, 1988), page 25.

28. Thomas Dubay, *Faith and Certitude* (San Francisco: Ignatius Press, 1985), page 15.

no matter how good and successful from the point of view of a generally acceptable idea of "goodness" and "success") can escape the really big questions: *What do I believe to be the absolute truth about my existence? What happens (if anything) after this life?*

Having reflected on questions of immortality at various points throughout my life, I have also tended (no doubt like many others) to resist or minimize or suppress the inclination to think harder through some of those more challenging and difficult questions that elude easy explanation—questions that have been going through my mind, especially in more recent years. I feel a lot like Rachel Evans, when she wrote: "I figured if God was real, then God didn't want the empty devotion of some shadow version of Rachel [or Sam], but rather my whole, integrated self. So I decided to face [the Bible] head-on, mind and heart fully engaged, willing to risk the loss of faith if that's where the search led."[29]

It is challenging, and somewhat frightening, to come to a place where one gives in to the impulse to think about and deal seriously with such questions—to be willing to face them head on, no matter where the search may lead, knowing that it will likely bring more hard questions than quick answers. That's because they are not the kinds of questions that lead to inner peace, serenity, and confidence. Rather, they tend to shake up our world, bringing with them a tendency to question whether we should even be asking such questions. There's a not-so-subtle voice inside saying "don't go there"; "keep those questions at a distance, safely stored in the recesses of your mind." There's a feeling of stepping out into unsafe territory. Yet you can't seem to stop yourself from going there because the questions don't go away. I'm sure I'm describing a state of mind that some of you find to be true for yourself. Such is where I find myself at what feels like the beginning of my senior years. And, perhaps surprisingly, although it can be a very lonely place, such is where I am content to be at this stage in my life.

---

29. Rachel Evans, *Inspired: Slaying Giants, Walking on Water, and Loving the Bible Again* (Nashville, TN: Nelson Books/HarperCollins, 2018), page 67.

One of the most helpful resources that I've recently encountered in helping me to work through the loneliness of dealing with these difficult questions is a book by Henri Nouwen, *Reaching Out: The Three Movements of the Spiritual Life*. In explaining the difference between loneliness and solitude, he writes:

> "Unless our questions, problems, and concerns are tested and matured in solitude, it is not realistic to expect answers that are really our own . . . We are constantly pulled away from our innermost self and encouraged to look for answers instead of listening to the questions."[30]

Nouwen's point is well taken—we tend to avoid entertaining and lingering over the gut-level questions that arise from within, and instead look for quick answers. Why? For one thing, we're easily distracted away from contemplative moments—it can get very lonely when you go inward to face your demons alone. But also, we're so fearful of the questions that we do everything we can to avoid the painful but necessary effort of defining and understanding them fully. But I assure you, there's no shortcut to getting past the hard questions in life. Avoidance doesn't work—it just prolongs our pursuit of a resolution. That's why my purpose in this book is to be honest and open about my theological questions, to not continue to be caught up in the ease of avoidance. My purpose is to search for truth in the only way it can be found—by challenging its claims head on, not backing down from asking the questions that arise naturally, not to fear the answers that those questions might lead to—answers that very well might shake the very foundations of what I have believed my entire life. As Romano Guardini wrote: "Since faith is life itself, life in the fullest sense, it must undergo repeated crises, crises which concern not merely a single part of man's life, but his whole nature—his mind and all his potentialities."[31]

---

30. Henry Nouwen, *Reaching Out: The Three Movements of the Spiritual Life* (New York: Doubleday, 1986), pages 40–41.

31. Romano Guardini, *The Faith and Modern Man* (New York: Pantheon Books, 1952), page 94.

In his book, *Honest To God*, John A. T. Robinson captures exactly what I am experiencing in my own life; it's so on-point for me that I'll quote him rather than put it in my own words, because I couldn't say it any better:

> Over the years a number of things have unaccountably rung a bell; various uncoordinated aspects of one's reading and experience have come to 'add up.' The inarticulate conviction forms within one that certain things are true or important. One may not grasp them fully or understand why they matter. One may not even welcome them. One simply knows that if one is to retain one's integrity one must come to terms with them. For if their priority is sensed and they are not attended to, then subtly other convictions begin to lose their power; one continues to trot these convictions out, one says one believes in them (and one does), but somehow they seem emptier . . . Then, equally, there are other things which have *not* rung a bell, certain areas of traditional Christian expression, which have evidently meant a great deal for most people but which have simply left one cold. The obvious conclusion is that this is due to one's own spiritual inadequacy.[32]

When we start out in life we acquire our beliefs from our parents. We trust as certainties the ideas and influences that are deposited over time into our consciousness. Gradually we begin to look at our world through our own experience. We become less trusting of what we are spoon-fed and more reliant on our own conclusions about life. Over time, our childlike faith, which trusted with little or no question, gives way to mature, independent critical thinking, and the certainties we had taken for granted lose their power over us as we begin to judge our world based on our own independently arrived-at conclusions. When our prior acquired certitudes merge with our self-attained ideas, we make choices about what (from our youthful innocence) to retain as truth and what (in our maturity) to let go of. In other words, those expressions of faith begin to develop into beliefs

---

32. A. T. Robinson, *Honest to God* (Philadelphia: Westminster Press, 1953), page 19.

as we determine to hold on to them and nourish them, or they lose their hold over us as we judge them to be improbable or unrealistic.[33]

To expand a bit on this idea of the development or progression from simple faith to belief, Harvey Cox describes three stages or phases that we progress through, both individually and corporately.[34] We start out in an "Age of Faith," which characterized the early church as well as new believers. This initial phase is characterized by hope and mystery. As long as that mystery remains alive and evokes meaning and progress in one's walk, it remains dynamic and life-giving. But if meaning fails to materialize out of that mystery, faith will wane and eventually die, since we can only live with the fascination and awe of mystery for so long before it will either fade away as fanciful wishful thinking or prove to be genuine and therefore lead to deeper significance.

Next in Harvey Cox's scheme is the "Age of Belief" (corresponding corporately to the medieval church). For individuals, it is when we believe something to be true not just out of our childlike faith, but because we come to trust the church authority that pronounces it as truth (what Cox refers to as "prescribed doctrines"). In the larger (corporate) body of the church, faith progresses to belief as heresies and schisms arise, leading to the formation of creeds and hierarchies to combat those schisms and causing churches and denominations to *choose* what to believe and what to discard. The big question that follows, of course, is how to distinguish what is pure and original from what came in later and detracted from that pure and original form. In fact, we see this happening even in the New Testament, in Acts 15, when Peter and Paul sharply disagreed on a matter of observance. As individuals, we are influenced not only by what we deem (out of our own reasoning) to be worthy of belief, but also what we are persuaded to believe under the influence of those who help shape our lives.

---

33. See Peter Kreeft's book, *Making Choices: Practical Wisdom for Everyday Moral Decisions* (Ann Arbor, MI: Servant Books, 1990). Kreeft deals with the questions regarding moral decision making in this practical and readable book.

34. Harvey Cox, *The Future of Faith* (New York: HarperCollins, 2009).

Finally comes the "Age of the Spirit," in which one's focus turns outward, to social issues. This is characterized by a practical outworking of one's faith, rather than an assent to a prescribed body of belief, where Christians are less driven by theological questions, and more interested in social issues: justice, poverty relief, and so on.

In short, what seems to be emerging from this cycle of "faith-belief-spirit" is the sense that the ideal for a society (as for individuals) is to revert back from an age of belief to a more original age of faith, when the earliest church was characterized by a community of believers who were concerned with the practical outworking of their faith, rather than the deep questions that occupied scholars and students of theology through the long age of belief.

In the context of what I am saying in this book, our journey through starting out with innocent (and perhaps blind) faith, through the process of formulating beliefs, then striving to live in the spirit of that original faith is a journey of discovering how to make sense of our world. What I'm claiming is that the journey doesn't (or shouldn't) end at a certain level of maturation. More to the point I am making in this book, when it comes to theological convictions, while it is good and proper to stand firm on some undisputable issues, to become settled and stale in one's convictions to the point of intractability in the light of questions and doubts leads to a stifling and unproductive condition.

How is faith a journey?

Before going into some detail about my own faith journey, I should say a few words about the question, Why describe my story as a "faith journey"? When I look at life—my lifetime—in relation to eternity, it seems most like a journey. We travel through the stages of life toward a destination. In relation to the timeline that we are born into, it is a short journey, an instant in time (let alone an instant in eternity), although there are periods of the journey that seem long and arduous. It only begins to feel short as we come nearer to the destination, as a runner "feels" the end of the race coming the closer she gets to the finish line. (If you're a distance runner, you know how good that feels.) Frederick Buechner says it well:

> The journey is primarily "a journey in search." Each must say for himself what he searches for, and there will be as many answers as there are searchers, but perhaps there are certain general answers that will do for us all. We search for a self to be. We search for other selves to love. We search for work to do. And since even when to one degree or another we find these things, we find also that there is still something crucial missing which we have not found, we search for that unfound thing too, even though we do not know its name or where it is to be found or even if it is to be found at all.[35]

So if life is a "journey in search," a journey toward a destination, whether or not that destination is firmly fixed in your mind, what is the most important way to describe that journey? How do we walk through that journey without getting lost along the way? How do we navigate and interpret the unexpected forks in the road, the mistakes and misjudgments, distractions, failures, and sins—anything that would divert us from the proper path of our journey through life and cause us to lose our way?

Our humanistic culture conditions us to believe that our proper destination is all about our personal legacy—that which, representing the very best of our humanity, we deposit into the lives and memories of those we leave behind. This is true whether we strive for a successful career, a résumé of academic achievement, a memorable contribution to society, or satisfying relationships with spouse, children, friends. Do these define a successful life journey? To an extent, of course they do. But what is the one worthwhile end that an individual should strive for more than anything else in this brief and fleeting journey through life? What makes a life "successful"?

I would claim that the most important legacy we can strive for—indeed the only truly worthy motive in our journey through life, the only motive

---

35. Frederick Buechner, *The Sacred Journey: A Memoir of Early Days* (New York: HarperCollins, 1982), page 58.

that is of any real and eternal consequence, is <u>our journey of faith</u>. Please don't hear what I'm not saying—as I just noted, our accomplishments and achievements in life are certainly significant and should hopefully have meaning that extends beyond our lifetime. And the cumulative achievements of our life do determine and define our legacy. Of course I want to leave my children and grandchildren with not only good memories of life lived together, but with valuable lessons that will guide them through their own life journeys. And of course it is natural for us to strive to accomplish some good that will be remembered and be of benefit to our world, no matter what the scale of that influence. But here's the point: Assuming that there is a life beyond this life, my legacy finds its ultimate meaning only insofar as it has affected the eternal souls of those I've left behind. And let's face it—no matter what our life's achievements might have been, unless we've lived a very public life, a generation or two after we're gone we're forgotten. That's why we need to be constantly reminded about the inestimable and lasting value of depositing our very best into the people in our lives who outlive us. Even as I write that, I feel the loss of missed opportunities, which is why we need constant reminders.

What is a successful faith journey?

Let me state the obvious: Since a journey is merely a route toward a destination, it can reasonably be said that its success can most accurately be judged if and when the desired destination is reached. In the context of this book, I am putting forth the idea that one's faith journey encompasses the life and experiences of the individual for the purpose of arriving at a destination that is characterized by a living and active faith that brings with it consequences beyond one's own lifetime. That is how I would define a "successful" faith journey.

So the success of my journey of faith—at least my own criteria for considering it a success—will be more than a legacy of temporal accomplishments. And my journey, if considered a failure, will perhaps be more sternly judged than to have been merely a life of missed opportunities. If and when I meet God face to face, will He judge my life based on my incremental successes and failures? If He does, I'm in trouble, for my past (and future) failures outweigh (by any measure) any successes I might have achieved (or will achieve).

God's purpose for my life??

Rather, I find it comforting (whether it's realistic or not) to hold to the biblical perspective that my existence has meaning only insofar as I fulfill God's ultimate purpose for my particular life. In his book *The Adventure of Living*, Paul Tournier writes of the events in life, that it is not ". . . a matter of knowing whether they are fortunate or unfortunate, whether they are favorable or unfavorable to us, whether they constitute a success or a failure, but rather of what they signify in God's purpose."[36] In other words, the meaning of my life is measured not so much by my incremental failures and successes, but by how I cooperated (or failed to cooperate) with the purpose for which I was privileged to have lived. That is why I say that the most important aspect of the journey through life is one's faith journey.

But let's define that most important journey through life: our "journey of faith." What is faith? I posited a definition of faith earlier, but let's look at a more authoritative definition. The Bible defines faith as something of "substance," a real entity; firmness; being sure. But a substance that consists of what? Again, the Bible gives the answer: hope. *"Now faith is the substance of things hoped for . . ."* (Hebrews 11:1). In other words, according to the biblical perspective, the things that we hope for in life are true (have real substance) only in relation to the degree of our faith. So the level of our faith is a real force that actually has the power to determine our hopes or fulfill our aspirations, just as the woman's faith in Mark 5 (referenced earlier) brought hope that was effective to heal her.

Now let's take it a step further. What is the one thing that, without exception, every individual who has ever lived or will live hopes for more than anything else, even if he or she wouldn't admit it? Simple—an afterlife, that his or her life will extend beyond death. (If you deny this, try thinking of one thing that would be more precious to you than that.)

I do not hope for this

---

36. Paul Tournier, *The Adventure of Living* (New York: Harper & Row, 1965), page 52.

So we're all on a journey through this temporal existence, which will end. But (working from the presumption that this journey is only the first leg of an eternal journey) before we come to our life's end, we have an obligation that we can't escape—either we work to make our individual journey meaningful or we don't. Either way, assuming there is a God and assuming we have an eternal soul that will live on after this body of flesh is no more, there must be eternal consequences to how we walk through this journey of life. That is why I revolve my story around the idea of a faith journey. What could possibly be more important for others to know about me? With that in mind, I can't think of a more appropriate question to ask myself than this: What makes my life journey a success? *yes this is the question*

So let me dive right in by talking about what I believe to be the rudimentary element of the journey, what I would call the starting point, and what is, for me, perhaps the journey's most challenging struggle: my struggle through the process of thinking about the idea of "simple faith."

Is simple faith good enough?

A story in the Gospel of Mark that has always stood out to me as a very moving narrative is Mark 9:24, where the father of a suffering son petitions Jesus to deliver his son of a demonic possession. Jesus is about to grant the father's petition and heal the son's condition, but before he does so, he puts a test to the boy's father to see if he has faith to see the miracle materialize. Jesus essentially challenges the father (v. 23), testing his level of belief: "All things are possible to one who believes." *really!*

Without hesitation, the father responds: *"Lord I believe, help me in my unbelief."* As a father myself, I am deeply moved by the blunt honesty of this father's confession. *my statement!*

If I were to briefly characterize my spiritual journey I would say that it has been, and continues to be, a struggle through questioning, uncertainty, periods of doubt, and even, at times, outright unbelief. But at the same time (for reasons that I hope are becoming clear), my journey has been one that I can best describe as a fight to hold on to my faith, if at times only by a thread (like the wavering faith of the father in Mark 9). I wrote about this several years ago in response to a published article on the subject of faith, when I was struggling through a particularly difficult season in my journey (see my letter to the editor of an archaeology magazine titled "The Thread becomes Stronger"[37] in Selected Writings).

Again, perhaps I'm not so different from many Evangelicals who would say they struggle with faith. So my story, my spiritual journey, continues on a steady trajectory through spiritual experiences that will hopefully bring progressively more certainty and perhaps more satisfaction or resolve in my faith, even as I continue to fight to believe and to hold on to my faith. If you haven't given up on reading this book by now, you might have started to gain a personal sense of that struggle, and perhaps also a seed of hope that underlies the struggle. So let's move on, and see where it goes.

Can faith exist with doubt?

I have often thought about where I would hope to be at the end of my spiritual journey, and what would be an ideal ending to my life story. Perhaps the best conclusion would be for me to finally come to the point where I enjoy a simple faith, an unwavering faith that is free from doubt, an absolute and unquestioning commitment to the authority and inerrancy of Scripture, and resolute, persevering trust that God is in sovereign control over my life—in short, that I would be a model Evangelical Christian.

The truth is, I'm not sure whether my faith will ever be unwavering, or to put it more bluntly, I doubt if my faith will ever be *simple*. Furthermore, as I've come to realize (and in fact become comfortable with), nor do I any longer aspire to that kind of "simple faith," for reasons that I hope are becoming clear. On the contrary, I would claim that a spiritual journey that is completely free of doubt is not necessarily a quality of a stronger or more robust faith (although neither would I claim it is necessarily a weaker faith), but it can in fact be a shallow and unthoughtful journey of faith. Again, I'm certainly not claiming that a completely secure and unwavering

---

37. Samuel Cardillo, "The Thread Becomes Stronger" in *Biblical Archaeological Review*, 2007.

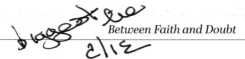
faith is not true faith. Of course it can be, and is, for some people. We have all known people in our lives who do have that kind of faith—my own mother comes to mind. I'm not claiming that a simple, or childlike, faith is not a profound faith. Of course it is, and in one respect, simple faith is the greatest kind of faith since it has the power to produce the greatest results. As Jesus put it, *"Whatever you ask in prayer you will receive if you have faith."* (Matthew 21:22). No doubt that's a big "if." It doesn't allow for the slightest doubt if it is to produce results. In my experience, the reality is that there are a great many Christians (perhaps even in my Evangelical circles) who, for the sake of maintaining an inner sense and a public aura of spiritual well-being, simply reject doubts when they arise or choose not to deal with doubts. I don't fault them if their well-being demands that they live in avoidance of doubt. For me, it simply doesn't work because it's not honest.

A few years ago I came across a stirring book, *Learn to Grow Old* by Paul Tournier, in which he expresses this conflict that we Evangelical Christians experience between faith and doubt. Tournier captures this tension perfectly for me. In his last chapter, in the context of a discussion about accepting death, he writes:

> If I am asked, "Can you, in faith, accept death?" I cannot honestly reply anything other than "Yes and no." What a contradiction! . . . But the contradiction lies at the heart of our human nature. Can one accept anything without repressing some rebellion? . . . Can one never utter a yes without repressing a no, or a no without repressing a yes? *Can one say "I have faith" without repressing doubts, or can one talk of one's doubts without by that very fact expressing one's faith? Does not faith consist most of all in recognizing that one lacks it? . . . I have sometimes got to the point of admitting my perplexity and my incapacity to say clearly whether I have faith or not.* (emphasis added)[38]

I have come to that point of perplexity many times. Faith, to me, is a lifelong struggle between the dual nature of who I am innately (that is, my

---

38. Paul Tournier, *Learn To Grow Old* (New York: Harper & Row, 1972), page 228.

nature as conditioned from birth), with a natural inclination to doubt, and a spiritual inclination to believe, conditioned by my exposure to and adherence to biblical faith. As Rosemary Ruether pointed out, faith is indeed a challenging journey:

> Charting one's journey of faith is always a precarious business . . . We are always in mid-journey as we go through life . . . we are always reassessing our past experiences and reflections in the light of new challenges. A side journey in our spiritual progress, one temporarily shelved, might suddenly become urgent again.[39]

So, rather than talk about my journey as a complete story, as if I'd attained a higher level of spiritual maturity (as I think I've made clear, I hold out little hope that this will happen in my lifetime), I've decided to tell my story now, in the midst of my questioning and doubting, because I think it's more useful and more genuine to tell my story as an ongoing account of one's unique struggle to go on in the faith, but much more than that—to discover if there is a way to prosper in my faith journey despite not having "arrived." I find encouragement in the words of Christian philosopher Gabriel Marcel, who came to faith later in life after what he describes as a "winding and intricate journey." As he explains, he did not regret that journey:

> . . . for many reasons and especially because I can still recall it vividly enough to feel a particular sympathy with those who are yet on the road, following out, often with great difficulty, tracks resembling those which I stumbled along in my time.[40]

One of my criticisms of Evangelical Christianity is that we as a group manage to convince ourselves that, considering the alternative, this matter of faith makes complete sense; that it is all utterly rational and the alternative (unbelief) is completely irrational; that doubt is the enemy of faith; and

---

39. Rosemary Ruether, *Disputed Questions: On Being a Christian* (Ossining, NY: Orbis Books, 1989), page 11.

40. Gabriel Marcel, *Being and Having* (London, UK: The Dacre Press, 1949), page 203.

that the strength of one's conviction about the veracity of Scripture and spiritual matters is a true and accurate measure of the maturity of one's faith level. But in fact, not all of us who identify as Evangelicals have the luxury of having such a simple, unquestioning, and unthoughtful mindset and experience. Or as Hans Küng put it, "The faith of a rational human being should at least not be irrational . . . Christian faith is a faith to be rationally understood and justified."[41]

As someone who is deeply enmeshed in this battle against the impulse to accede blindly to the simplistic mindset that I just described, I hope that my own experience might be useful to those who find themselves in a place similar to my own—a place that I would describe as persistent spiritual dissatisfaction, discomfort, striving at times to accept "the whole package" of traditional or Evangelical Christian biblical understanding, yet struggling to accept certain parts of the package that don't make sense; and still (perhaps most importantly of all) being comfortable with, and even embracing that struggle and that process! It's one of the underlying questions I hope this book is addressing: Is it possible to flourish as a Christian believer in such a condition as I've just described?

Evangelicalism or Fundamentalism?

I've already used the term "Evangelical Christianity" a few times. Let me pause and point out what I believe is an important distinction between Evangelicalism and its more toxic corollary, Christian Fundamentalism, within the context of my faith journey. Evangelicals and Fundamentalists hold certain beliefs in common, namely, the authority and veracity of the Bible and most emphatically the gospel message of the substitutionary atonement of Jesus Christ as presented in the New Testament (the reality of the "born-again" religious experience).

Fundamentalism goes a step beyond Evangelicalism. As a reactionary movement that evolved in the second half of the 19th century, it arose in reaction to the progressive ideas that were taking shape, most notably the

---

41. Hans Küng, *On Being a Christian* (New York: Doubleday & Co., 1968), page 162.

"higher criticism" of the Bible and the advance of the evolutionary theory of human origins—ideas that challenged the miraculous nature of God's intervention in human affairs. *what are God's intervention in human affairs*

Fundamentalists hold rigidly to a literal interpretation of Scripture in its entirety. For example, against all scientific evidence to the contrary, they consider the Bible a dependable source for geology or biology. Fundamentalists also accept as factual historical data every word of Scripture, including even the most fantastic narratives. Consequently, Fundamentalism is, without apology, a more separatist position than Evangelicalism. In addition, Fundamentalism thrives in an environment in which persuasiveness is key. In what Richard Holloway describes as "intellectual slavery,"[42] believers must be so firm and settled in their theological position that they are able to persuade others of the correctness of their belief, so the power of persuasion is more important than the factual truthfulness or scientific basis underlying the belief system. And as long as adherence to the underlying truthfulness of the belief system remains intact, the claims maintain their authoritative status.

In my experience growing up in the faith, from my youth up through the 1970s, when I attended Bible college, my friends and I would have characterized ourselves (unfortunately with a warped sense of pride) more as Fundamentalists than Evangelicals. Why? I think it's because we grew up in a subculture in which we were conditioned to separate ourselves from worldly influences, establishing barriers to distinguish ourselves as "true believers," and indeed, regarded ourselves as possessing the right theological positions, in contrast to other ("wrong") Christian groups. It was basically a mindset of "us against them." (To give you a sense of what that divide looks like, there is a strong connection between this phenomenon and the rift that exists in today's "Trump era" in the American political scene, between conservatives and liberals.)

---

42. Richard Holloway, *Godless Morality* (Edinburgh, Scotland: Canongate Books, Ltd., 1999), pages 11–12.

The problem was that we adopted strong positions on issues that really didn't matter at all. It was considered a badge of honor to hold unwaveringly to the idea that our doctrinal position was the one and only "correct" position among all other Christian denominations. We were convinced that all other interpretations of the sacred text were faulty. That mindset didn't provide the space to encourage us to think for ourselves and outside of that fundamentalist box.

To be clear, that's not to downplay what I still hold to as some of the core issues that concern (and to a large extent) define Fundamentalists, although I hold them more loosely than I used to. Rather, it is the unpleasant and harmful baggage that comes with the label (including its politicization) that alienates Fundamentalist tendencies as marginal. In fact, I don't think it is an exaggeration to say that when it comes down to it, hardcore Fundamentalists tend to be preoccupied with the political and social hot-button issues, like abortion and gay marriage, almost to the exclusion of anything else. And when those religiously oriented concerns bleed into one's cultural and political views, to the exclusion (or at least marginalization) of all other issues, we end up with a situation like that in our current social and political environment—where our country is so deeply divided that one wonders if the damage is beyond repair.

Since we are living in an era in which politics so often bleeds into religion, if I may be permitted a slight diversion (and please skip over the next two paragraphs if you are uninterested in what you might consider irrelevant to the subject at hand), it is deeply troubling that for the first time in my memory we are living in a political environment where a president regularly and freely expresses utter contempt and disdain for an entire political party—virtually half of the population—a party whose people he represents but also resents. Surely it must be evident to both conservative and liberal alike that the ultraconservative position he takes on the kinds of issues that divide us is all for the sake of political expediency, not at all based on personal religious conviction.

I bring that up because I think many of us long to see a day when political affiliation won't be the litmus test to judge whether one is an Evangelical

Christian or not; a day when it will not be strange to hear someone refer to him- or herself as being on the "religious left." As Bianca Vivion Brooks recently wrote in an opinion piece in *The New York Times*, "To take on the Religious Right, we need a Religious Left . . . My faith shapes my progressive politics. I wish this were true of more liberals" (*The New York Times*, November 21, 2019). I hope we will soon come to a place in this country where we will stop defining one another's faith perspective with reference to a single issue or two that happen to push the wrong buttons, and that we won't allow ourselves to be so easily alienated from people with whom, despite our differences, we would otherwise carry on meaningful dialogue and relationship.

As simplistic as it sounds, I believe that the current state of social sickness that we face today in our relationships with one another in this divided country can be healed by resisting the temptation to express contempt over our differences long enough to have meaningful dialogue, listen, and seek to understand the other's point of view. Although I think this need for healing applies to both sides, I do find it ironic that the conservative or "right" element in this country—the political party that used to pride itself on holding the moral and religious high ground, and, all evidence to the contrary, still does hold to that opinion of itself—has in fact evolved to become a party characterized largely by spite, mockery, and disdain. In his recent article dealing with the movement of conservatives away from their traditional values, Michael Gerson wrote that ". . . one of the most extraordinary developments of recent political history is the loyal adherence of religious conservatives to Donald Trump . . . whose Christian beliefs could hardly be more incompatible with traditional Christian models of life and leadership." He goes on to say that "the corruption of a religious tradition by politics is tragic," pointing out that "the evangelical political agenda has been narrowed by its supremely reactive nature." He describes how Evangelicalism devolved from its former adherence to traditional religious values to become a Christian political movement in which Christian theology is emphatically not the primary motivating factor.[43]

---

43. Michael Gerson, "The Last Temptation," in *The Atlantic* (April 2018). https://www.theatlantic.com/magazine/archive/2018/04/the-last-temptation/554066/.

But back to my point: What I just described was not how we conducted ourselves back in those days—rather, we were fixated on our Fundamentalism. Aptly, the subtitle of Peter Berger's book, *In Praise of Doubt*, is "How to Have Convictions Without Becoming a Fanatic." Some of us still haven't figured this out. Berger deals with the phenomenon of Fundamentalism at length. He points out that there are two basic requirements imposed by Fundamentalists: First, that "there must be no significant communication with outsiders." Second, that "there must be no doubt." His first point, of course, highlights a prevailing attitude in some Evangelical environments that should, of course, be dismissed as pure nonsense (seclusion is a primary characteristic of cultism).

But Berger's second point is sobering and certainly merits serious consideration for many Fundamentalist Christians. Rejection of all doubt about the core principles of the faith characterized my own spiritual journey through my earlier years, but I have come to find such a narrow view completely untenable. Berger shows how the Fundamentalist mentality deals with doubts by attributing to them a negative status, and ultimately, to rebellion against God. As he puts it, Fundamentalism seeks to create solidarity based on a coerced uniformity of beliefs and values among its members. This mindset is quite understandable. Belonging to a group of like-minded people creates a support system that is essential to our well-being. In other words, "you are who you hang with." But more than that, the Fundamentalist mentality is driven by fear of the consequences of not holding to the "right" belief system. That's why the "hellfire and brimstone" style of preaching of Puritanical theologians, such as Jonathan Edwards and George Whitefield, held sway among Fundamentalists (and still does to an extent, although in a toned-down language and delivery).

Peter Berger has argued that (notwithstanding Christianity's generally suspicious attitude toward the idea of pluralism) there are certain benefits to religious pluralism, one of which is that it "influences individual believers and religious communities to distinguish between the core of their faith and less central elements."[44] Berger suggests that in the interest of sharing

---

44. Peter Berger, "The Good of Religious Pluralism," *First Things*, April 2016, page 42.

common strengths or even for the sake of constructive interaction with other faith traditions, why not compromise on nonessential elements that cause division, while maintaining the core essentials as nonnegotiable? He points to another benefit of pluralism, which resonates with me in my personal journey—that it has the potential to persuade one from taking his or her faith for granted. As Berger writes: "The loss of certainty is of course disturbing. But it is a good thing if one values deliberate and reflective assent as a component of authentic faith."[45] I find this reasoning to be more and more convincing and enriching (not to mention less exclusive) as I distance myself from conventional Evangelical thinking. As Brian McLaren noted, those who find themselves in a place of growing doubt about their faith will eventually realize that "the search for authentic faith must be the most life-changing quest anyone can ever launch."

Sebastian Castello, an opponent of John Calvin, captured the core of my thinking about the problem of doubt when he argued in his treatise, "The Art of Doubt, Faith, Ignorance, and Knowledge" (1563), that certain biblical passages are hard to believe; but rather than give up on the possibility of coming to a correct understanding of such texts, if we do the hard work of exercising our minds, the doubt and uncertainty that we experience can pay off by paving the way to knowledge and truth. There is a mindset that characterizes Evangelical Christianity that goes something like this: One should not burden oneself with uncertainty; we should accept uncritically all of Scripture and what others (i.e., the professional clergy) present as the "proper" interpretation of Scripture; and we should reject input from anyone who holds a divergent view. I am well familiar with this mindset, as it was my own way of thinking before I started examining the Bible and faith on more than a surface level. This mindset can't allow doubt to arise because there is an all-or-nothing mentality—either every word of Scripture is true or none of Scripture can be relied upon. This either/or, all-or-nothing, dualistic mindset stifles our natural inclination to ask questions or challenge the sacred text, solely because it *is* sacred, and therefore beyond questioning.

---

45. Ibid.

* * *

Having presented a rather lengthy account of some general and prelim-
inary ideas and questions that characterize a faith journey, I will now go
into some detail by looking at the practical ways those questions have been
(and are being) worked out in my own journey.

PART TWO

My Faith Journey

"The way I figure, there ain't no use for a fellow going out looking for religion; It's well . . .it's just got to come to a fellow."

(Alvin York, in *Sergeant York*)

"The weight of your silence is terrible. I pray, but I'm lost, or am I just praying to nothing? Nothing, because you are not there."

(Father Rodriguez, in *Silence*)

The Risk of Openness About a Faith Journey

I have a keen sense of the risk I'm taking, going out on a limb and talking about my particular journey of struggle for a life of faith. Until now, I have hesitated to talk much about my faith journey, primarily for the sake of my intimate circle of family and friends. Here's what I mean: When my children were young, it was vitally important to me (right or wrong) to show strength of conviction in spiritual and religious matters so that I would not influence them to unbelief, as if my own certainty about an absolute system of belief were persuasive enough to influence the faith of my children. As I imagine is the case in other religious traditions, as Evangelicals, we are conditioned to guide our children toward embracing our faith. I had never wavered in my conviction about the *importance*, even the necessity, of faith for myself and my loved ones. So naturally I had always strived to exemplify, as best I could, the life of faith for my children. But to be convinced of the *importance of having* faith is not the same as *having* faith. I don't believe that one can have an active and vibrant faith by simply making a choice to embrace it when it ceases to be compelling, although some would argue the opposite—that embracing faith is a choice that one can make in a purely objective way. As my favorite author Peter Kreeft expressed it:

> We must choose either to believe or not to believe. The third option is a fake. Not to choose is to choose to say no. There seem to be three options: (1) to choose good, (2) to choose evil, and (3) not to choose . . . But (3) is often really the same as (2) when it is due not to ignorance but to refusal.[46]

Admittedly this is a gray area, a matter of personal conviction that can't be proven one way or the other. After all, is it not the very nature of religious conviction that its verifiability or "truthfulness" is unprovable? Or as Hans Küng put it: "If it [faith] could be proved, it would no longer be faith."[47]

---

46. Peter Kreeft, *Making Choices* (Ann Arbor, MI: Servant Books, 1990), page 16.

47. Hans Küng, *On Being a Christian* (New York: Doubleday, 1976).

faith tradition

I am often reminded of a conversation I used to have with a Jewish co-worker who was brought up in a nonreligious home. She insisted that—had I been brought up in her home—I would not have had the support system to embrace the religious background that I grew up with, and had she been born into my family, she would have had religious grounding. And therefore, if conditions of our upbringing were different than they were, neither of us would necessarily hold to the viewpoints we were conditioned to embrace. It is, of course, a very reasonable argument for one's conformity or nonconformity to a faith tradition. It causes one to consider the tenuous nature of belief, that it is, in most cases, purely a matter of family upbringing.

Chad vs Hillary

This points to a very interesting and important question in the context of any discussion of a "faith tradition." One simply cannot sidestep the question: When and how does one's faith, which was passed on from one's parents, older siblings, mentors, and others become his or her *own* faith, rather than simply preconditioned by circumstances?

But to my point: In any case, I realize that I tread on sensitive ground in expressing my uncertainty. But I've also hesitated to talk about my personal faith struggles because I've always wanted to avoid the risk of having a negative impact on the faith of fellow believing Christians, again because—in spite of the weakness of my own personal faith—I have always considered faith to be *that* important.[48] Also, to be honest, I fear the consequences of shaking up the perceptions that my fellow believers, with whom I share life, might have of me. And (even more frankly) since I have, at least until now, been most comfortable with and feel most at home in the world of Evangelical Christianity and have usually been willing to serve in the church in the capacities for which I may be gifted to serve, the reality is that by exposing my doubts I am no longer considered to be qualified to

---

48. Here's one of those areas where I mentioned my thinking might be seen as being contradictory. If (as I believe) faith *is* vitally important, it might seem dishonest for me to, at the same time, deny others the opportunity to observe my struggle for that faith. If the quest for faith involves such struggle, why not have the courage to work out that struggle instead of internalizing the struggle? In other words, perhaps an open display of honest struggle is more beneficial to family and friends than an internalization of that struggle. I leave it as an open question.

fill certain roles as I was when I was "solid" in my faith. Incidentally, I don't argue against the wisdom of that way of thinking on the part of church leadership. In fact, I agree with it, which is why I recently withdrew voluntarily from a track toward ordination as a pastor.

Along with that, I've experienced another interesting and somewhat troubling phenomenon that comes into play when you expose your detachment from the faith you once held strongly: People who once trusted and respected you *because of* your conformity to their beliefs now worry about your spiritual condition and become alienated and distanced from you because you are no longer "trustworthy" as a fellow Christian companion. It's not intentional, and no one is to be blamed for the distance created. It's just that the spiritual or theological differences that now separate you create a divide, a corresponding interpersonal disconnection between you and your fellow Christians. You're simply no longer considered as trustworthy as a spiritual advisor or counselor as you were when your faith was vibrant, or at least committed.

In my case, one church leader with whom I had developed a strong and trusting relationship actually expressed to my daughter a fear for the "trajectory of my faith" as I distanced myself from the theological positions held by that particular church. In other words, that individual—and others who knew me prior to my revelation of experiencing a faith crisis—drew a conclusion that downgraded my level of reliability as a trusted companion, advisor, and co-Christian. My honest, thoughtful, and heart-rending distancing from my formerly solidly held faith came with a corresponding diminishment of my trustworthiness. That's the power of a faith community!

Desiring Faith versus Having Faith

On the positive side, I would confess that I feel like the character Fox Mulder in *The X-Files,* who, when faced with unsolvable mysteries, is asked "So you believe in these things?" and responds "I want to believe."

I *want* to have faith. I regard faith as a vital ingredient in my journey. And I'm most gratified for at least that desire. In fact, I can't imagine living life without that purposeful desire to strive for faith. To me that *striving* is as important (if not more important) than arriving at a doubt-free, unquestioning faith.

That mindset seems counterintuitive because the idea of continual striving for something that seems out of reach is not an inclination that normally strikes one as a productive or fruitful activity. But when it comes to faith, there must be a basis for holding on, even—or especially—in the face of the seeming impossibility of attaining it. As I understand the nature of faith, it is to be always trusting, hoping, striving, pressing in on, but not necessarily achieving, a full understanding. For once we've "achieved" faith (whatever that means, and if it's even possible), would a vibrant faith really be necessary any longer? So that simple but profound appeal of the unnamed father to Jesus in Mark 9:24 *("Lord I believe, help me in my unbelief.")* captures my own personal appeal.

The Problem Of Relating to a "Hidden" God

Before I elaborate about some of the particulars of my own journey of faith, I should make one more point about how Christians would describe what it means to be in relationship with God, which will shed light on my story. In my Evangelical circles, it has always been a clear notion that in order to flourish as a Christian, one must experience a personal relationship with God. The phrase "a relationship with God," while well-known and common in Christian circles, is found nowhere in the New Testament. But it is, in fact, one of the core expressions Christians use to describe the way in which a believer connects with or interacts with God.

But I would suggest that it is, in fact, not completely fair to talk about one's connection with God in terms of a "relationship," for the following reason: It goes without saying that the nature of a working relationship is that two sides must actually meet and interact. When discernible interaction doesn't happen—in spite of the pursuit of one party toward the other, perhaps over the course of several decades, perhaps over a lifetime—is it not justifiable to regard that as a one-sided relationship, and therefore dysfunctional? But since I don't personally know a single committed or dedicated believer who would admit that his or her relationship with God is one-sided (or dysfunctional), I have to ask: What is it that gives the typical believer confidence that God is actually paying any attention to him or her? How does one know, in the face of God's seeming distance, silence, unresponsiveness, and even absence, that his prayers are even being heard? What constitutes meaningful interaction with God? How does one find reconciliation between the two completely opposing scriptural truths represented by the following two biblical texts?

"Seek and you will find; knock, and the door will be opened."

(Matthew 7:7)

"Why, O Lord, do you stand far off? Why do you hide yourself in times of trouble?"

(Psalm 10:1)

The focus of Evangelical Christianity has narrowed down and individualized the gospel story to the point where it focuses on what Brian McLaren calls a "framing story," a story that sees individuals as being born into a doomed world, in need of individual rescue from our hopeless state. Rather than seeing the story as a universal and all-encompassing, interactive relationship between the Creator and His creation as a whole, the story narrows down to a situation where Jesus came to appease God's wrath for the sins of certain individuals. While no gospel-oriented Christian would dare to admit it, it is certainly the conventional Evangelical view that there's no hope for us as a civilization. Rather, salvation is narrowed down to a rescue operation for individuals who are fortunate enough to have heard, been moved by, and ultimately responded to the gospel message, and therefore are a part that body of believers who are saved from God's wrath and will be rescued out of the horrific devastation that will characterize the End of Days.

It boils down to a legal transaction rather than a transformative, collective human experience. No action on the part of the recipient is required, except an assent to the legal transaction. Sure, there are expectations on the part of the recipient that follow the redemptive experience, but when considered as such (as a sort of "rescue operation"), the whole matter of "personal salvation" becomes quite self-serving and individualized, rather than constituting a larger, all-encompassing, universally beneficial act of God on behalf of all of creation. In other words, the offer of personal salvation—salvation narrowed down to a personalized and individualized transaction over against a communal and all-encompassing design of a beneficent God—brings to mind the idea of a God who acts toward His creation based on a sense of selectivity and even discrimination.

Now, no one would deny that a one-sided relationship, a relationship characterized by unreciprocated love, is an unhealthy and unprosperous relationship. Obviously, it takes two engaged parties to sustain a thriving relationship. In pointing out the difference between dependency and love, best-selling author and psychologist Scott Peck defines dependency as "the inability to experience wholeness or to function adequately without the certainty that one is being actively cared for by another."[49] Love always pursues the other; dependency is always seeking to be pursued where love is absent. But there is a typical Evangelical argument that goes something like this: Like a loving and attentive parent toward a wayward child, God is always in pursuit of a relationship with His children, even when they walk away. It isn't the parent who is to blame when the child walks away, but the child who has chosen to be unresponsive to the parent's love. In the same way, so the argument goes, it's my fault if I feel estranged from God in the face of His relentless pursuit of me. I don't do my part in responding to the God whom I am conditioned to see as a loving and patient father because that's what the Bible says about Him. *questionable argument*

That is a solid argument as far as the biblical evidence presents it, but faulty on the practical level. Again, the pursuit of a loving Father is clear to the child. He doesn't just say the right words; he *acts* like a Father; He involves himself in the life and activities of his child, so that there is clear evidence of His love. When the child walks away, the Father (if He is truly loving toward the wayward son) pursues relentlessly, face to face. But if the Father

---

49. Scott Peck, *The Road Less Traveled* (New York: Simon & Schuster, 1978), page 98.

is silent, *hidden* as it were, what basis is there for the child to reciprocate? Since the premise of the argument in defense of God is that He is always in pursuit, whether or not we sense it or believe it, the only logical conclusion is that we (the pursued children) haven't done our part in responding and reaching out to the God, whom we are conditioned to see as a loving and patient Father. So, the argument goes, to blame God is unjustified.

Granted, because I'm a flawed parent, my pursuit of my children is far from consistent and far from justifiably reciprocated. But is it not the ideal (nor should it be the ideal) as with the parent/child pattern, that the parent—the pursuer, the initiator of the benevolent act—is the one who naturally takes the initiative to pursue the child?

And so with God's pursuit of us—His children—we're conditioned to immerse ourselves in Scripture in order to grasp the nature of God's being and character, so that we can become more and more convinced that the God of that Scripture is always seeking to come into a deeper relationship with His people. Why? Because we take God at His word. But do mere words on a page prove the love of an otherwise absent pursuer? And yet, the biblical record speaks of real historical evidences of a God who pursues—the account of Saul/Paul in Acts 9 comes to mind immediately—where God arrests Saul, who is on his way to instigate a persecution of Christians, stops him dead in his tracks, and turns him completely around, suddenly and dramatically changing the heart of this hate-filled and murdering villain into a dedicated and effective servant. There's also the famous parable of the Father's pursuit of His wayward son who, contrary to any reasonable expectation, returns to his Father (Luke 15), a story that should move the heart of any parent.

So Scripture gives us a conflicting picture of a God who, out of love for His creation, expresses a desire to pursue His wayward children at any cost, but at the same time, for whatever reason, hides that tendency or seems to make it difficult—one might even say impossible—for us to detect that desire. The mystery of the Hiddenness of God has been dealt with extensively, and it can be articulated in different ways. But basically it comes down to the question: "If God is good, why doesn't He make it more obvious?"

major question

Does God hide Himself for our benefit? Is our conception of a "hidden God" misplaced, and in reality God is not hiding Himself? Is it that we're just not perceptive enough to recognize His involvement? If God is capable of being known and wants to be known by His creation, both of which are revealed truths in Scriptures, such as Proverbs 8:17 ("I love those who love me, and those who seek me find me"), why doesn't He make that happen in an unambiguous way? Howard-Snyder and Moser summarize this problem in their introduction to *The Hiddenness of God* like this:

> The potential for crisis arises [in that] Jewish and Christian theists believe that their flourishing as persons depends on their being in a personal and social relationship with God. For many such theists, however, there is no such discernible relationship. God is hidden, if not in fact at least in their experience . . . God seems too hidden to care at all . . . Despair over life itself is, then, a natural result of divine hiddenness.[50]   *despair*

Howard-Snyder and Moser go on to say that if the seeming absence of God persists, there is potential for "frustration and, eventually, bitterness and despair. Trust in God then crumbles . . . and trust in the hidden God often seems the only reasonable option . . ."

To be honest, even from my youth, my notion (and indeed my experience) of God's hiddenness has been my greatest hindrance to accepting and responding to the prospect or reality of His care for or attention to me personally. As a "good" Christian I, like so many others, have conditioned myself to pay lip service to the idea of the presence and involvement of a living and loving God in my life, but not because it is a reality for me. On the contrary, my experience of God's absence has been the dominant feature of my relationship with God. Like others, I suspect, I have felt as if I have always "worshipped God from afar," rather than having a true sense of connection. This is not so unlike the experience of the Israelite elders in Exodus 24, who were sternly instructed "not to come near," as only Moses was

---

50. Howard-Snyder and Moser, *Divine Hiddenness* (Edinburgh, Scotland: Cambridge University Press, 2002), page 2.

permitted to do, but rather to maintain their distance from God for fear of His holiness and majesty. It is with that sense of distance and estrangement from God that I now turn to a brief account of my own spiritual journey.

The Phases of My Faith Journey

Journey through Childhood and Youth

Until the summer of 1984, I could best describe my spiritual journey as one of accepting blindly and uncritically the religious teaching that I had received in my childhood from my parents and Sunday school teachers, through my church youth experience, and through four years of an Evangelical Bible college education. I don't recall going through any significant periods of doubt concerning the core traditional Evangelical beliefs—that the God of Scripture is the Creator and sustainer of all that exists, that the Bible is God's holy word as it was transmitted through the inspired biblical writers and preserved in the form that we have it today in the Hebrew and Greek texts. I believed in the dual nature of man as mortal body and soul/spirit, and thus I believed that all of humanity is destined for an eternal "afterlife"; and I believed that the only way to be acceptable to God was through Jesus's substitutionary and atoning death and His bodily resurrection.

In my childhood and youth, I accepted those elements of faith as my core belief system, as absolute truths, not because I had reasoned for myself on my own initiative through the relevant doctrinal and biblical questions, but because I didn't have any reason to be challenged to think any differently than how I was taught. My childhood and youth were characterized by generally uninspired religious and spiritual indifference, interspersed with periods of what seemed to be revivals of interest in spiritual matters here and there. It was the usual Evangelical upbringing of Sunday school, youth group meetings and activities, and generally a life secluded from secular (or as we labeled it, "worldly") adventure. Sadly, even through four years of Bible college, I had little interest in spiritual matters, happy to coast along in my circle of Christian friends and activities while maintaining a safe distance from the "unregenerate" world around me, and along with that, a comfortable distance from God as well.

As for my relationships during those years, my closest friend through junior high and high school was David. We met in seventh grade when, as I recall, we showed up at band tryouts together with our trumpets. That was the beginning of a close friendship that lasted into our college years. We would spend hours drinking 5-cent cups of coffee at the local mall, listening to new Chicago albums as they were released, and just spending most of our after-school hours together. I loved going to his house and just hanging out with his family because he had a lot of siblings and there was always activity around his house. From time to time, David and I would engage in heavy theological discussions as if we knew what we were talking about. He always aspired to be a pastor (which in fact he is to this day). He was known as the "reverend" (or the "rev") in high school. As I think back, my friendship with David was one of the catalysts that stirred me to start thinking more seriously about my faith.

Another outstanding memory of my youth occurred between 1971 and 1974, when I spent my summers on the staff of Harvey Cedars Summer Camp. While I have full and fond memories of those summers and the friendships that were formed living and working with 40 or so teenagers, looking back at myself during those summers now as an adult, I regret that I wasn't more conscientious about taking advantage of the opportunity to develop a greater level of maturity. In general, we had little guidance when it came to relationships. We were never discouraged from dating at what was obviously too early an age. When I was growing up in Evangelical circles in the late 1960s and early 1970s, it wasn't unusual for Christian youth to get into relationships with each other, to "go steady," and these relationships were created within the circle of our youth groups. During those years, relationships were dissolved almost as quickly and easily as they were established. Consequently, we as Christian youth went into and out of relationships casually. This forging and breaking of relationships no doubt brought with it emotional baggage that I think had a lasting impact on my ability to discern what a serious and healthy relationship would look like later in life.

I also wonder what it would have looked like for me to have been more serious about my life's direction when I was going through those carefree and careless teenage years. There's much to learn by thinking back to ways that some of the adults in my life interacted with me during my youth. I remember only one couple, Steve and Cathy B., who took the time to speak to my life in a serious way, while some of the other adults I related to seemed either aloof and out of touch with the struggles of a shy teenager, and therefore kept their distance, or other adults who were overly eager to relate to me on my own immature level rather than encourage me to rise to their level. But those few relationships with some wise older people in my life inspired me to make it my purpose to be more conscientious in relating to younger people in my own sphere now.

Academic journey

In spite of my generally useless college experience, there was one high point (well, two, if I include meeting the love of my life), but in relation to the direction my spiritual journey would take, there was an important connection made, which really salvaged my college experience, and in fact made it worthwhile, and in the most unlikely of circumstances. For some reason, in my third year I decided to fill an elective slot by taking a course in biblical Hebrew. The professor was Austin Potts, who, though he was a brilliant scholar, was generally thought by most students to be, well, let's just say not the most interesting professor to listen to. (Rumor had it that he actually had his "jokes" written into his lecture notes. So during his lectures he would say, in his characteristic stiff manner, "Now I must tell a joke . . .") But humorless though he was, it was through his influence and guidance that I discovered that, not only did I have an aptitude for learning Hebrew, but I actually enjoyed the class and found my niche in the study of biblical Hebrew. Up to that point in my education, I was really an average student. I realize now that that was because I simply wasn't interested enough in any of the material to be motivated to apply myself to serious study. As I recall now, that was the first time I achieved academically without much effort. For several months after I graduated, during the fall of 1977, I studied privately with Dr. Potts, who was gracious to tutor me once a week at his home. These sessions were invaluable in feeding my desire to learn the language, and it was during that time that I became aware that I was heading toward a life of study of the Hebrew Bible and related areas.

Debbie and I were married the year after I graduated, in 1978, and spent a couple of years enjoying our new life in Richfield, Debbie's hometown. I worked at her father's lumber mill, and she worked at the local sewing factory. I was living an ordinary but rather dull life of hard work, quiet evenings, and no serious obligations. It was an inconspicuous life, simple and boring. My job consisted mostly of stacking boards from one pile to another—eight hours a day of mindless, brain-numbing, torturous labor. To this day, whenever I express boredom with the routine of life, Debbie reminds me of how I would come home from the sawmill and agonize over the excruciatingly monotonous day that I had just had, only to be repeated the next day.

After a year or so, my unrest at being intellectually stale drove us to move to my hometown in New Jersey, as if for some reason that would relieve my boredom. But I was desperate—any change that would take me away from that torture chamber of the sawmill would suffice. We got involved in the local church I grew up in, and I took a job in a woodworking shop. Woodworking later became my lifelong hobby (ironically, since I hated my sawmill experience). It was a good-paying job, which allowed us to save enough money for our next big venture: a year in Israel.

Journey to Israel

Despite a change in physical circumstances, I continued to be drawn toward academic pursuit. I decided to apply to a program for Hebrew studies at the Institute of Holy Land Studies in Jerusalem, and we moved to Israel in the summer of 1980. It was an unforgettable year in every respect, not least because it solidified my resolve to pursue my Hebrew studies and also inspired a lifelong interest in areas related to biblical studies (biblical geography, archaeology, church history).

The core of the program of study revolved around field trips concentrated around a regional division of the land of the Bible. Each trip was preceded by a comprehensive study of the particular region, including geopolitical, social, and historical backgrounds. On-site lectures and discussions highlighted and illustrated the biblical events. It's been more than 35 years, and I still see in my mind's eye the physical settings of the stories I read in the Bible. The program was led by Jim Monson, who was as passionate about the Land of Israel as he was about his teaching. He became a mentor and friend to me while we were there and for years after we returned home. Indeed, it was Jim who taught me to create and preserve visual memories, not through the lens of a camera, but through nature's perfect lens—the eye. Jim taught me to "look along" a vista (to use Peter Kreeft's phrase) rather than just to look "at" a landscape, to see the whole panorama of a physical setting, not just to stare at an end point. Whenever I think of that, I can't help but remember that comical scene from *National Lampoon's Vacation*, where Chevy Chase drives his family to the Grand Canyon, only to look out at the stunning panorama for a few seconds, then get back in the car and drive off to the next tourist trap: (https://www.youtube.com/watch?v=AqNwo2NpmGY). Anyway, Jim was one of those rare gems who come along only once or twice in a person's lifetime—the kind of mentor who invades the comfortable way of seeing life that you think you are satisfied with, someone who enlarges your world, who changes or redirects you to see what you didn't see in your world before. We carried on a meaningful correspondence after I returned to the States, which helped me to stay focused for some time afterward.

When I returned to the U.S. in 1981 with a master's degree in Hebrew (a year that I recall to this day as a highlight of our early years of marriage), we found ourselves resuming life just as we had left it a year earlier—in the absence of a tangible plan, we moved back to Richfield, and I worked, once again, at my father-in-law's lumber mill. This was a year of confusion and, to a large degree, a sense of failure. I wondered what I was doing back in the same old routine as before Israel, and although I was able to use my newly acquired learning to teach classes and preach a few sermons at the local church we attended (Richfield Mennonite), I was restless and frustrated about the repeated cycle of my own indecision. I wondered if my life would amount to anything. But thankfully, the desire to study never completely left me, and after a few months of drudgery and indecision I decided to make a permanent break from my humdrum, directionless life and pursue doctoral studies.

Journey through a challenge to my faith

We moved back to Philadelphia, and I enrolled in Dropsie University in 1984, which brings me to what really is the beginning of my journey through spiritual challenge. My first year at Dropsie marked a major shift in my life's direction. So significant was this chapter in my life that it stands out as the most important turning point, for I came to discover a new world of learning that would dramatically change the way I would view God, the Bible, faith, and everything I had come to embrace as solid foundations of my spiritual journey in an unquestioning way up until that point. I embarked on a new and invigorating journey into the world of critical biblical scholarship. It was exhilarating—it opened up a whole new world of knowledge that was unlike anything I had pursued up to that point, and for the first time in my academic life I was driven to pursue my studies relentlessly in my new field of biblical scholarship.

I remember my first day in Hebrew language class, when my teacher, an Orthodox rabbi who has since become a colleague and close friend, said to me in front of the class something like, "I hear you have a good background in biblical Hebrew." I remember thinking proudly that I was about to prove how right he was. I was eager to pour myself into my studies, determined to become a professor of Hebrew Bible.

But my newly discovered passion to learn came with disturbing consequences to my faith. Before I knew what was happening, I began to entertain questions that I had not—up to that time—allowed to enter my mind. Previously, I was blissfully avoiding the hard questions about faith—questions that no doubt had occurred to me from time to time but were better left unasked because if I were to bring them to the surface and probe into them, I felt I would be drawn down a road that I was not prepared to deal with intellectually, spiritually, or emotionally. While I had not abandoned my Christian faith, my thinking at that time was perhaps something like what C. S. Lewis expressed when he wrote those chilling words: "I ceased to be a Christian." . . . "From the tyrannous noon of revelation I passed into the cool evening of Higher Thought, where there was nothing to be obeyed, and nothing to be believed except what was either comforting or exciting."[51] In my case, uncertainty and skepticism grew incrementally, so subtly in fact that I wasn't aware of some of the compromises in my thinking, until I realized that my faith had begun to erode.

Compromise is defined as an agreement reached by adjustment of conflicting or opposing claims or principles. By definition, it is a gradual process, which is what makes it so difficult to detect in ourselves. Two opposing claims converge in the mind. Both claims have merit, and both are equally appealing, although in opposition against each other, pulling one's mind and heart in opposite directions. Unwilling to let go of either influence, I began to rationalize how I might harmonize the two influences, how I could entertain the new thing that was drawing me while retaining the old intact. This is where the mind becomes remarkably creative. One starts justifying elements of the new by talking oneself into the idea that maybe the old ideas were slightly flawed, perhaps outdated, and therefore not 100 percent correct at every point.

After that, it seems reasonable to detect the possibility of a flaw in the authority behind the former claim, and before you know it, the erosion is well underway. But surely it's justified. After all, we reason, we desire truth above all else. And certainly, if we should discover a weakness in our former code of values, isn't it a step forward to adjust our convictions accordingly? As we embrace the opposing "truth" by building further justification of its merit, the old truth (while still, although weakly, tugging at our heart because, after all, it sustained and satisfied us for so many years) diminishes in its value to the mind and heart. Finally, it graciously bows out, for it has lost the battle and no longer has the will to fight for supremacy in our thought.)

---

51. C. S. Lewis, *Surprised by Joy: The Shape of My Early Life* (New York: Harcourt Brace & Co., 1955), pages 58–60.

For me, the two "opposing truths" were (1) the old certainty that that the Bible is God's inerrant word dictated to the biblical writers by God, transmitted literally as absolute truth to be received in every detail; and (2) the new assumption that the Bible is a text that was "perhaps" inspired by God and given to man. (There's my first compromise: I wasn't quite willing to deny divine inspiration altogether, but it was not necessarily completely trustworthy as the authoritative word of God since it was transmitted through the flawed biblical writers—that was my second compromise). From there it was an easy and natural step for me to question my faith in the divine authority of Scripture.

As it happened (fortuitously perhaps), life didn't quite follow the academic course that I had plotted out for myself. The class I entered with, in 1984, was the last class of students who would enter Dropsie. The school was founded in 1907 as a Jewish institution of higher learning and historically maintained a small student body of mostly Jewish students training to be rabbis or professors in Jewish institutions. In the years leading up to my enrollment in the school, increasing numbers of Christian students were doing their doctoral work there, which meant less financial support from the world of Jewish philanthropy. In fact, my class consisted entirely of Christians, without a single Jewish student. We were a small group of about eight students, some already pastors of Evangelical churches, some training to be pastors, and the rest of us looking toward careers in academe. In part because of the non-enrollment of Jewish students, and partly because Dropsie could no longer compete with other developing programs of Semitic studies offered at other institutions, it became clear sometime during the end of my first year that the school could no longer sustain itself financially and wouldn't last much longer.

In my second year I took a part-time job in the Dropsie library in order to earn some needed money as Debbie and I were getting ready to bring our son Joseph into the world. During that first term of my second year, it became a settled matter—Dropsie would shut its doors permanently at the end of that semester. But out of that closure, the chairman of Dropsie's board, with the support of philanthropist and diplomat Walter Annenberg, orchestrated the founding of the Annenberg Research Institute, a center dedicated to the advanced study of Judaism. I was offered a full-time job in the newly established institute, which started in 1987. Five years later, in 1992, the Annenberg Institute merged into the University of Pennsylvania and was renamed the Center for Judaic Studies (later to become the Herbert D. Katz Center for Advanced Judaic Studies), where I took the position of administrator. Thirty years later I am still in that position.

So here I am, more than three decades after I began my studies at Dropsie, still working through the same questions that I began to struggle with in my first year in 1984. As I've said, I tried through the intervening years (for the most part) to avoid troubling my family and friends with my struggle. Again, this is because I've always felt that I should show a sense of confidence to those around me, as if this were a sign of strength. I wonder now if this mindset of suppression has been the best way for me to deal with my doubts with my family and friends. While it might have served to avoid difficult dialogue and unnecessary confusion on their part, perhaps it would have been better for them to see me dealing honestly with my questions and doubts.

Before going into more detail about my particular faith struggles, I would like to mention briefly another struggle that Debbie and I faced through the first seven years of our marriage. Since we both grew up in families with multiple siblings, we had a similar desire to have a large family. But that was not to be. When Joseph finally came along in 1985 (seven years after we got married), we thought we were finally on our way to creating that big family. But we waited another eight years for Zoe—so very well worth the wait! So although that big family we both imagined for ourselves was not to be, from the day Joseph and Zoe were born until now, I feel unbelievably fortunate to have two amazing children, without whom I could not imagine living life. Joseph and his wife Rachel have given us four amazing grandchildren, with whom we are hopelessly in love, and Zoe and Dante (her first and only love) have blessed us with two grandchildren who are a joy beyond words. What could be better?

While, until a few years ago, I had generally kept my doubts about spiritual matters to myself, I have at certain times talked freely about some of my struggles with doubt. I mentioned above that I wrote a letter that was published in *The Biblical Archaeologist* magazine in 2007, in which I reacted to an article written by a biblical scholar who had lost his faith because, after studying the Bible critically for many years, he concluded that faith was too irrational (see "The Thread Becomes Stronger" in Selected Writings at the end of this book). That article hit home for me in a powerful way at the time since I was struggling with the same questions of faith because of my studies, and I was particularly moved to respond in some way to what he was saying. But interestingly enough, my reaction was a defense of "sticking with the faith" rather than abandonment. As I reflect now, many years later, on what I was going through at the time, I realize that I was fighting a battle against my own inclination to draw away from my faith. Looking back now at what I wrote (12 years ago), I believe, as I did then, that faith, in order to be an active, genuine faith, must be, by nature, difficult. If I can lose my faith simply because it no longer seems completely rational, perhaps it isn't true faith and isn't worth fighting for. Now as I look back some 30 years after my graduate school experience, although my grasp on faith is still tenuous, I am still grateful that somehow, in the face of erosion and doubt, I have been spared from complete abandonment of my faith. I'll explore this struggle in greater depth later in this book.

* * *

The first couple of years of the 1990s marked another turbulent period in my spiritual journey. We were living in a suburb of Philadelphia, and I was working at the Center for Judaic Studies and teaching Bible and archaeology courses in the adult education program at Philadelphia Biblical University. I was still holding out the prospect of having a career in academia, but I was gradually losing hope of fulfillment of that dream, as my eroding Evangelical certitude (not to mention the practical demands of life) were closing in on me. Joseph was five years old and one of the few joys of my life as I entered another spiritual drought. We attended a local Baptist church in a Philadelphia suburb for a few months but found no spiritual refreshment there.

We started attending services at Tenth Presbyterian Church in Center City Philadelphia, where we soon felt comfortable and got involved in children's ministry. We had good memories of Tenth Church, as that was where we had attended church during our college years. But again, I was experiencing spiritual drought, content to be going through the motions of living a life of faith but without much of the genuine reality.

Journey through "brain death" and back

As much as I would like to avoid writing about this phase of my journey, I can't sidestep it if my story is to be completely transparent and honest. Around the same time I was experiencing the unrest described just above, we reestablished contact with our best friends from college (and our life-long friends), John and Judy, who invited us to an event at Philadelphia's Civic Center, where we heard a charismatic preacher named Larry Lee. Having grown up in a mainline denomination, neither of us had been exposed to the captivating style of preaching that we heard that night. We were enthralled by his preaching because it reached deeply into the spiritual drought that we were living through. And so, we were introduced into the world of Charismatic Christianity. At first it made me uncomfortable because, while I had always known about the phenomenon, I had never taken it to be a serious branch of Christianity. But now it seemed to be reaching a part of me that was in need of something more alive, more meaningful, as a way to experience the life of faith that had been eluding me for so long.

I had always found it hard to get past the physical displays of emotion that characterize Pentecostal or Charismatic worship practices, some of which were just downright laughable to someone like me, who has always been skeptical of phony theatrics. But there was another side of the emotional expression that attracted me in my deadened spiritual state. It was almost as though I thought it acceptable to allow my dead soul to be energized and stirred up, to be demonstrative, to force the issue and act out a semblance of faith and commitment, to motivate myself to perform the "act" of worship, toward the end that maybe God would take notice of my effort and make it real.

In 1991 we started attending services at Living Waters Community Church, a Charismatic church whose membership consisted in large part of people who were (like us) broken and desperate for spiritual renewal. Perhaps I was genuinely, though subconsciously, identifying with that mindset of brokenness and desperation that seemed to fit right in with the general atmosphere of the people around me. Services typically revolved around a prolonged time of "praise and worship" music that became so popular in the 1980s and (generally) long sermons that focused on motivating folks by preaching hope for a better future. Therefore, much of the teaching revolved around the so-called biblical promises of God to restore to people what was lost through the various hardships many of the folks had faced. There was a regular diet of encouraging (extra-biblical and personalized) "words from God" that promised restoration of health, wealth, and overall better times ahead. Scripture was used as well, but grossly out of context. Every promise or blessing of God made to any and every individual or group in the Bible was fair game to be applied to us.

Since I was coming into that experience from a state of spiritual deadness, "charismania" (a word that does not appear in standard English dictionaries, but which I see as a very good description of the phenomenon) was an experience that, at first, appealed to me because of the spiritual drought that I was experiencing. It was invigorating to find an outlet that allowed for, and indeed encouraged, an expression of my renewed faith. But it was unsustainable.

Within a year or so it grew shallow and unsatisfying as I sensed the lack of theological depth, not to mention the overuse and outright misuse and misapplication of biblical and theological truth. Based on hype, it played on the emotions and felt needs of the congregants. It focused on the individual as recipient of physical, financial, and emotional well-being. God was more or less the "instrument" (a genie in the bottle so to speak) through whom these benefits came. This is because the Charismatic encounter revolves around the experience of an encounter with the living God to the exclusion of anything that would interfere with, or be outside of, that personal generating experience. The preaching holds the attention of the people because it is always upbeat, always promising blessing and relief from life's pressures. Thinking had to give way to experiencing because God speaks to our hearts, not to our heads. The preaching was "fiery but fluffy."

Soon it became unbearable, to the point where I couldn't take it anymore. I remember sitting in the chair during services, wishing I could be somewhere else, anywhere else, while people around me were singing and praying for all they were worth. I wondered what they were thinking about my obviously lousy attitude. I think I was hoping that if I just waited it out the "spirit would move me" to experience God's presence. It didn't. So I sat. But I sat defiantly. I really can't remember a period of time when I was more out of tune with life, angry at myself, at Debbie, and at God, than those few months. They were months of pure internal agony.

Finally, one Sunday I announced to Debbie that I would not be going to church that morning. Debbie continued attending, and the weeks that followed marked a low point in our marriage. I found myself, for about a month of Sundays, sitting mindlessly in a small local Presbyterian church on Main Street in Williamstown, among a group of 30 or so people who, it seemed, were as uninterested in church as I was. In the meantime, the other "single" women back at Living Waters were encouraging Debbie to keep attending the church without me and see to her own spiritual well-being. That made me even angrier. I had no desire or motivation to pursue spiritual matters, and I know that my family suffered for my lack of interest during that dreadful period.

I actually did have one interesting encounter just before we left Living Waters that really helped confirm in my own mind my decision to leave the movement. Lew, the music director at the church, had become a good friend. We had spent about a year playing music together on the worship team, and he, better than anyone else, seemed to understand what I was going through because he, too, was a thoughtful person. We would have some really good conversations about the nature of the church life that we were a part of. I believe Lew understood my problem better than anyone else at the time. What I most appreciated about Lew was that unlike me, he was able to overlook what I considered to be the weirdness and shallowness

of the theatrics because he had (and to my
the people who were drawn to a church lik

During a chance encounter with Lew severa
on our time at Living Waters, and he made a
vation when he said: "Sam, it's a hospital," b
restoration or emotional healing for people
of spiritual drought. I admire his outlook an   .... appreciated
his determination and ability to stay committed to helping people who
are drawn to that kind of ministry—people who are perhaps intellectually
lazy but psychologically sensitive enough to recognize their spiritual needs.
Maybe, I'm the one who is in greater need since I didn't (and no doubt still
don't fully) recognize my spiritual insensitivity. But we'll get to that . . .

But back to the encounter I just mentioned—I think it was 1996 or 1997—
Lew invited me to have lunch with him and Pastor Dan. I knew it would
be their last-ditch effort to keep me connected to the church. I realized
that they truly did care for me, and I appreciate that to this day. I laid out
my thoughts and feelings bluntly and honestly. They kindly reached out to
me, asking me to stay in spite of what I was experiencing, trying hard to
convince me that it would be fine if I would just exercise patience and allow God to move in my heart and draw me back. But I was convinced that
it wouldn't be fine. I was finished with that phase of my spiritual journey,
and I wasn't to be persuaded otherwise. When we parted ways, that was the
last time I would speak to Dan. Lew and I tried to, or at least purposed to,
maintain a level of friendship for a while.

Over the years since we left Living Waters, I have often thought about how
much I regret going through that experience during the early 1990s. While
I still believe (somewhere in the recesses of my mind) that God, in some
fashion, exercises control of the course that our lives take, I also think that
we make choices that are contrary to God's best course of action, but that
He redeems our mistakes. The mystery of the interaction between divine
sovereignty and free will is one that I find impossible to reconcile.

that we make choices that are 100 percent free. (I'll say
this later.) So my choices and their consequences during those
a continuing source of regret. I realize this is an extreme and per-
somewhat unfortunate point of view, but the way I often think of it
w, as I look back, is that I went through a period of voluntarily experiencing a sort of "brain death" for those few years. And I do feel something
of a sense of loss of some important years of parenting, when Joseph was
going through some difficult preteen years and Zoe was in the prime of
childhood. Thankfully, in spite of that, we did immensely enjoy life as a
young family, and we have wonderful memories, but I do regret lost opportunities with our children and ways that I could have done a better job
at parenting than I did, if I had been more conscientious. This confession
is hard for me to express, and it still causes me some degree of sorrow and
regret. But at the same time it is gratifying to watch my kids parent their
own children in ways that I had failed. And I do, thankfully, feel a sense
of "having a second chance" to help raise the grandchildren, whom I love
dearly, by actively involving myself in their lives.

Another turning point in my spiritual journey was in 2006 when some
friends invited us to attend a church service. We were involved as members
of Sovereign Grace Church in Marlton for eight years. Sovereign Grace
Church reinvigorated my spiritual journey as I rediscovered what "church
life" was supposed to be all about—a community of believers who are passionate about finding the meaning of life through an understanding and
serious expression of biblical truth. But my spiritual journey was to take
even more twists and turns in the coming years.

Journey through sickness

In the fall of 2008 I developed a skin disease, which, by the spring of 2009,
progressed into a full-blown case of psoriatic arthritis. Within a matter of
weeks, it spread over my entire body from head to toe, to the point that I
couldn't get out of bed without severe pain in my legs. When I finally went
to my doctor, he immediately sent me to a dermatologist for a consulta-
tion. I started a treatment of strong doses of a medication, the side effects
of which (including suicidal thoughts) were almost worse than the disease.

I stopped taking the meds a few days after I started, flushed them down the toilet, went on a raw food diet for several weeks, and gradually settled into what became a year-long treatment through diet alone, which brought me back to full health. (That's another story that I won't go into here.) But in the meantime, I spent the fall and winter of 2009 sitting and lying on the couch wrapped in blankets because I was constantly freezing. I would leave a trail of dead skin everywhere I went around the house, and I spent hours each night sitting in a hot tub, which was my only relief from constant itching and pain. I would crawl into bed at night and wonder if the nightmare would ever end. Debbie was especially caring during that time, helping me in ways for which I will always be grateful.

During the months while I was sick, I read and wrote. For some reason (to this day I still don't quite know why) I sat down one day and wrote a 10-page paper on the Christian radio preacher Harold Camping. I had known about his weird teachings about the end of the world because, while I was growing up, the radio in our home was always tuned to his station. His teaching had evolved into more and more bizarre ideas over the years, and recently, just a few years before he died, he was off the wall with his ideas about biblical numerology and the end of the church. And since his mantra would always drive me crazy, and since I had nothing better to do, I sat down one day and wrote this paper. Reading and writing on the couch or in bed were my only activities. I mention that story to show how my attitudes toward the irrational features of my faith affected the development of my cynical attitudes toward Evangelicalism.

But more to the point, one day during my illness I picked up a book that had been sitting on my shelf for I don't know how long, entitled *The Case for Faith*, in which Lee Strobel confronts a series of "objections" to faith, like the ones I had been experiencing over the past 20 to 25 years. One chapter in particular caught my attention, "Objection #1: Since Evil and Suffering Exist, a Loving God Cannot," in which Strobel presented his interview with Catholic philosopher Peter Kreeft. Having grown up in the faith, I had the typical Evangelical understanding of how God and evil could coexist. My theology taught me that God had created a perfect world and sinless humanity, but through humanity's inclination to sin, man rebelled against God and ruined God's perfect creation, thus reaping the consequences of living in a fallen world. I had what I considered a theologically sound understanding, but it wasn't satisfying in a practical way—it didn't make a difference in how I really felt deep down about the suffering I was experiencing. Even Job's three so-called friends had correct theology, but it was of no comfort to Job. For me too, right theology wasn't speaking to my need to be healed of this painful and drawn-out sickness. So I was intrigued by this particular chapter in Strobel's book because it spoke to my own suffering at the time.

Since my suffering seemed unbearable at times, I needed a better answer—a more personal answer—to the problem of pain. At the end of that chapter in Strobel's book, Kreeft says that "the ultimate answer [to pain and suffering] is Jesus's presence . . . When your world is rocked, you don't want philosophy or theology as much as you want the reality of Christ." He wrote that suffering brings us face to face with God, as it does in Job's experience, and so the answer to suffering is perhaps not finding that mysterious "something" that will bring understanding or satisfaction, but it is "*someone*." It is simply the answer to the basic but profound question we ask when we suffer: "Why, God?" or "Where are you, God?" When we ask those questions, it seems to me that we aren't really looking for explanations as much as we are desiring *presence.*

Peter Kreeft illustrates the point in a way that has always stuck with me. Our desire for the presence of God is like this: Imagine you are alone, in a broken-down car, in a blizzard, in the middle of nowhere, in the middle of the night, without a phone, miles from the nearest civilization—totally helpless, alone, and afraid. What you want most of all at that moment is for a friend to be there with you. I realized that I was craving God's "presence" as a satisfying response to my suffering, not just "right theology *about* God."

Getting one's theology right in the midst of real suffering is like offering a glass of water to a drowning man—it's a gross underestimation of the problem. Like Job, during that period, I was constantly asking the question "Why?" We find these "why" questions throughout Scripture: Moses asked *and then what*

God: "Why have you brought trouble on this people?" (Exodus 5..
David asked God the "why" questions over and over, for example in Psaln
10:1: "Why do you hide yourself in times of trouble?" Or in Psalm 42:9:
"Why have you forgotten me?" Those are not only good questions to ask
God, but they are the *right* questions. The point is not necessarily a matter
of getting an answer. Rather, the point is to cry out with the question, to
capture God's attention and let Him know that it's not okay. Life is painful
right now, and I want you to know that I'm not okay with it!

capture God's attention

I have come to believe that God isn't worried about what we might think
of Him in our worst hour. Jesus says to believers in Revelation 3:15-16: "I
wish that you were either hot or cold . . . because you are lukewarm I will
spew you out of my mouth." I've spent a lot of years being lukewarm (indifferent) in my relationship with God, and it never feels good. (Incidentally, Kreeft wrote an excellent little book on this topic called *Jesus Shock*,[52]
in which he fleshes out the idea of indifference in our walk of faith—the
simple but profound idea that ". . . if Christianity is true it should change
everything.") But what is the apostle John trying to convey in that statement in Revelation: "I wish you were either hot or cold?" The idea is that
indifference is the worst possible way for us to relate to God. Indifference
is revolting to a God who, when He calls me to Himself, demands that I
make a decision—yes or no. But certainly not "maybe," or "I'll see how
things go," or "if a better option doesn't present itself," or "not yet." I think
indifference is the absolute worst place I can be in my spiritual journey
because it's even harder to navigate through than outright denial. That,
incidentally, is another reason I've written this book—it's an outworking
of my battle against indifference.

But back to the question of suffering. My reading of that chapter in Strobel
led me to what would become a deep appreciation for Peter Kreeft's writing. He writes: "Only in a world where faith is difficult can faith exist . . .
Scripture describes God as a hidden God. You have to make an effort of

---

52. Peter Kreeft, *Jesus Shock* (South Bend, IN: St. Augustine's Press, 2008), page 40.

"[53] That line rings truer for me every time I read it! And : effort has to do with coming to grips with the problem . There is an important truth that Kreeft brought to my awareness... a logical and self-evident truth, namely that evil can only have any meaning in a world where there is also good. Because God is God and we are not, we can't understand His purposes, and when we face trials, we often wonder: "Can any good come out of this evil?" And here I will make a statement typical of Evangelical theology, which, for me, is more of a confessional question mark than something I'm ready to adopt as an absolute assertion of belief: Doesn't it seem likely that God is wise enough to allow evil when He foresees that a greater good will come out of it? In fact, do we not have the best example of this in the gospel story—the worst evil that was ever committed turned out to be the greatest good that was ever accomplished? When Jesus was crucified, His disciples were devastated. They had staked their entire lives on His promise as the only hope to bring deliverance. It seemed to them that His plan had ended in utter failure, until they realized that the evil perpetrated against Jesus turned out to be the means of salvation to the world!

In any case, I went on to read Kreeft's book *Making Sense Out of Suffering*, then C. S. Lewis's *The Problem of Pain*. Both books helped me endure the constant pain of my sickness. I found out quickly that Kreeft is prolific. He has written some 40 books and presented numerous lectures on philosophical topics ranging from proofs for God's existence to wide-ranging subjects, such as suffering, heaven and hell, angels, sex, and biblical and theological works, all of which fascinated me and occupied me for the next few years.

The Main Point: Fighting The War Against Doubt

I mention my time reading Kreeft and Lewis because they gave me a gift, which I badly needed at a crucial point in my spiritual journey, when I could have easily been tempted to throw the whole faith package out the

---

53. Lee Strobel, *The Case for Faith: A Journalist Investigates the Toughest Objections to Christianity* (Grand Rapids, MI: Zondervan Publishing, 2008), page 33.

window. They helped me gradually realize and accept (*and this is really the main point of this book*) that the fight for faith is not a single battle to be fought and won once and for all, but a lifelong war that is made up of a series of battles day in and day out, some won, but many lost, throughout a lifetime. I no longer believe, as I used to, that faith necessarily increases in proportion to how much one desires it, or cultivates it, or how much one immerses oneself in the biblical teaching on faith. No matter how hard one works to achieve it, faith can be elusive.

Why can I make that claim? Simply because that has been my experience. Nor do I believe that once a plateau of faith is reached, it naturally becomes a bedrock of fidelity in one's standing. Faith is not an acquisition that, once achieved, necessarily remains solid. It's not a baseline upon which one builds into a deeper faith. Rather, as I stated at the beginning of this book, the faith battle rages on and on, at least in my own life, even as I write. But I'm learning that, while the battles along the way are painful, overall it's not an arduous war. It's a necessary war, win, lose or draw. It's a war that I would not choose to avoid. It's not a war that always has to feel like I'm resisting God and facing God's resistance to me, although at times it *is* that.

There are two aspects of every war, whether it's an individual internal conflict or a world war between nations: a positive aspect and a negative. Whenever we fight, we are fighting at the same time *for* something and *against* something else; *for* freedom and *against* tyranny; or in the case of an individual spiritual battle, like the one I'm describing in this book, *for* inner peace and assurance and *against* doubt and unbelief.

Therefore, as I've come to realize, these struggles are not without their benefits and even their joys. The struggle to believe in God and grow in one's faith in God—rather than being something that happens spontaneously as one matures on his or her Christian walk—is a dynamic lifestyle, full of uncertainties, obstacles, struggles, ups and downs, questions with and without answers, and sometimes just plain confusion. Life in general presents us with a constant barrage of questions and uncertainties, some of which we resolve sooner, some later, and some never. Why should our journey of faith be any different?

I've come to realize that it's better to struggle with questions—real questions to which we often can't settle on immediate answers—than it is to never question, never doubt, and to always come to quick resolutions. How boring it would be to live life like that portrayed so dramatically by the character Truman Burbank (in the movie *The Truman Show*, before his dramatic "conversion experience," that is, before he realized that his whole life was just a television show to entertain viewers), a life free of tough choices, to never have to think deeply about life's deep questions. How utterly stagnant our spiritual development (not to mention our intellectual development) would become if we were to be satisfied with the same old worn-out arguments that perhaps satisfied us in the past, when we were spoon-fed truth, but that we continue to hold as absolute, no matter how vehemently our maturing spirit rebels against them. How arrogant it would be to always be sure that what we think and believe now will never be subject to challenge and change of heart. As Truman Burbank discovered when he realized his life was not his own, it is liberating to abandon the false security that served as a protective bubble consisting of an insincere faith claim and determine instead to live in light of the unknown and unknowable spiritual realities.

It's both interesting and exasperating to observe how some believing individuals use the language of faith in what seem (from the outside looking in) to be typical and simplistic ways. There's a customary and "proper" language and vocabulary that is typically used in communication with other fellow believers in delicate situations—a language that is both validating and, at the same time, not confrontational. These expressions, because they are overused in conversations between fellow believers, lose their power and ability to create a real sense of resolution, wonder, and newness with regard to the faith. If you've spent any time in conversation with Evangelical Christians, you will no doubt have heard (or even used) some of these expressions: "God is good"; "His ways are higher than our ways"; "God understands what you're going through"; "Be blessed"; and the number one go-to comment, which conveniently and safely concludes any difficult conversation with a fellow believer: "I'll pray for you." These and other typical comments, while well-meaning, are merely attempts to insert God into conversations that are difficult to navigate through in situations where you want to say what you really mean but are hesitant to do so because what you're really thinking would be judged as a faithless or "un-Christian" sentiment. And let's face it—while platitudes serve to make the giver of the cliché feel as if he's done his due diligence, they are generally unhelpful, convenient, and safe. We feel much better when we walk away from a difficult conversation with the idea that we've left the other party with a "godly" piece of advice, rather than a challenging or thought-provoking question or opinion.

Unexamined faith versus mature faith

In his book, *Socrates in the City*,[54] Eric Metaxas presents lectures from various theologians, philosophers, and educators. In his introduction to each lecture, he repeats the theme behind those lectures: Socrates's famous statement that that "The unexamined life is not worth living." Gregory Boyd applies Socrates's statement to faith: "Unexamined faith is not worth believing."[55] Both claims ring true. My own version of Socrates's claim is that unwavering faith, which, at least for me, has great potential to be "unexamined faith," is not necessarily a dynamic faith, and thus it's not true faith. In fact, I would say it's not even a virtue to be sought after. I don't doubt that for many it can be comfortable and satisfying to experience a lifelong, unwavering, and solid faith. But I would claim that it is not a disposition that makes one more spiritually mature in one's faith. As Romano Guardini put it: "A mature faith is a faith grounded not in enthusiasm and boundless expectation, but in steadfastness in the face of reality—a faith aware of difficulties and responsibilities, with a loyalty based not on emotions but on conviction and strength of mind."[56]

In his book, *Benefit of the Doubt*, Gregory Boyd argues that what he calls the "idol of certainty"—that thinking that sees the absence of doubt as virtue to be sought after—is not only unhealthy and unhelpful in one's

54. Eric Metaxas, *Socrates in the City: Conversations on Life, God, and Other Small Topics.* (New York: Dutton, 2011).

55. Gregory Boyd, *Benefit of the Doubt: Breaking The Idol of Certainty* (Grand Rapids, MI: Baker Books, 2013), page 47.

56. Romano Guardini, *The Faith and Modern Man* (New York: Pantheon Books, 1952), page 104.

spiritual progress through life, but it is an unbiblical idea. He shows how the Bible is full of stories of biblical characters who experienced doubt—serious doubt—and yet came to the point of being in vibrant relationship with God. Moses is a prime example of excessive doubt. In Exodus 4, right after he observes God's miracle of a burning bush that was not consumed by fire, Moses questions and doubts God's instructions no less than three times before he comes around to trust God (Exodus 3:13; 4:1; 4:10). Abraham is another example, as his doubt led him to dismiss God's promise of an heir through Sarah and take matters into his own hands. The Bible is, in fact, full of stories that make one wonder why God seems to have called the least likely (the doubters) to carry out His mission on earth. It makes one think that maybe, just maybe, it is the doubter, the questioner—rather than the person who acts out of his or her own self-confidence—whom God finds of interest to carry out His plans and programs for humanity.

But back to Gregory Boyd's point. I find great encouragement in his claim that to live free of doubt, never questioning or challenging God or the Bible, is really to live a thoughtless and stagnant spiritual life. In fact, strange as it may sound, I find that I appreciate the experience of dealing with internal spiritual conflict because it causes me to think more deeply about my fight for faith. I don't want to become lazy in my thought life, even if it means struggling with the inner turmoil. I want to be always in the posture of questioning and reexamining my understanding of spiritual matters because I believe the apostle Paul is right when he says: "The natural man cannot know the things of the spirit, for they are foolishness to him." So even though, as a believer, one takes on a spiritual nature, I believe, with orthodox Christian theology, that even while reconciled by God's grace, we retain our fallen human nature and, therefore, live in a dualistic condition of being constantly and hopelessly subject to reverting to natural thinking. That is why faith, inevitably, must always be a battle. It is the nature of who I am. The Apostle Paul knew this better than anyone (Romans 7).

what does it mean that God will

There is a certain confidence that should be active in my thought life—but it's a confidence that God will sustain me not *because* of my faith, but *in spite of* my *lack* of faith. In my view, God is not interested in how strong my faith is, but rather, in seeing my resolve to wrestle for my faith with all

Sustain me

my strength, just as He expressed approval with Jacob's persistent fight with the angel in Genesis 32, by granting him a blessing when He recognized that Jacob was not going to give up his struggle. What a reassuring story that is. Read it again—or for the first time if you haven't read it yet—and you'll see a vivid picture of the true character of a God who pays attention to those who fight for their faith. We see the same God answering David's persistent questioning of God's motives ("Why have you forgotten me?") instead of criticizing or correcting David (Psalms 42:9); and again in the book of Job, as God displays patience with Job, who rants and raves for 38 chapters before answering him. The lives of these and other biblical characters illustrate the benefits and rewards of being honest about one's doubts. Paul Tillich puts it this way:

> . . . for in the depth of every serious doubt and every despair of truth, the passion for truth is still at work. Don't give in too quickly to those who want to alleviate your anxiety about truth. Don't be seduced into a truth which is not really your truth, even if the seducer is your church . . . or your tradition.[57]

Job's story is particularly illuminating to me in fleshing out this idea of struggling with God. Throughout the narrative, Job presents a defense of his character in which he doesn't hesitate to challenge God and His reasons for allowing Job to suffer. "Does God not see my ways and count all my steps?" (Job 31:4) "Let me be weighed on honest scales, that God may know my integrity." (Job 31:6) Job questions God, and we're presented with the picture of a seemingly passive God, who allows him to go on for 38 chapters in incessant dialogue with his "companions," whose accusations serve only to set the stage for Job to state his case before (or more precisely, *against*) God. When God finally speaks, He addresses only Job, not the others, for Job was the only one who was serious enough to ask the tough questions, the honest questions, the right questions. These are questions, not religious platitudes, but the kinds of questions that can only come from one who thinks deeply, seriously, and honestly about faith and spiritual concerns. And in the end, God honors Job (not before He

---

57. Paul Tillich, *The New Being* (New York: Charles Scribner's Sons, 1955), page 67.

straightens out Job's faulty thinking about God's character). The narrative ends in a way that reveals God's pleasure with Job. So, in fact, God's question to Satan regarding Job's character at the beginning of the story ("Have you considered my servant Job, that there is none like him on the earth, a blameless and upright man, one who fears God and shuns evil?") is answered by God Himself at the end of the story when He addresses Job's false friends: "You have not spoken right, as my servant Job has." (42:7): *"For I will accept Job"* (v. 8).

I find a deep sense of satisfaction in the idea that God allows space for His people—space for me—to ask the questions that weigh on my mind. As is clear in the story of Job, and so many other biblical stories (Abraham doubting God's promise of an heir; Moses doubting his call; Jacob wrestling with God; Jeremiah complaining; and on and on), He patiently and kindly listens to our questions, doubts, and even complaints. As Boyd points out, even Jesus in His full humanity, in his deepest time of agony, expressed doubt and questioning—"If it be possible let this cup pass from my hand." While some, perhaps most, Evangelicals would portray those words as merely for our benefit ("Jesus didn't really mean it literally."), I would suggest that it would have been disingenuous for Jesus to have said that while not really meaning it in the deepest human sense. While the theological weight of that brief encounter between the suffering Jesus and God His father is difficult, if not impossible, to grasp, I can only see his words as a display of raw, human emotion—the genuine suffering of a human being in crisis. This is Jesus with His full humanity on display, while at the same time expressing the depth of sorrow at the thought of losing his eternal bond with God His Father.

What conclusion can be drawn from the realities of life that I've just described—that life consists of pain and suffering, confusion and doubt? Looking back, my particular experiences through academia, my missteps in denominational church experience, and my debilitating bout with my sickness were blessings in disguise, as they taught me some valuable lessons that would serve to sustain me in my journey toward faith.

PART THREE

Journey Toward Faith

"Try to be patient and courageous; patient in leaving the problem un-resolved for the time being, and courageous in not giving up the struggle for their final solution."

Viktor Frankl, *The Will to Meaning*

Questioning Foundations Of The Faith

I've intentionally titled this last part "Journey Toward Faith," rather than concluding with the idea of "arrival" at a posture of faith. As is evident by now, I haven't "arrived," and as I've tried to make clear above, I believe that as people of faith, we generally move in and out of faith throughout our lifetimes, as we progress on a journey toward faith. That's why I talk about faith as a journey, not a destination or an "acquisition." As I see it, the question *What do I believe to be the absolute truth?* takes on relevance most poignantly in the context of religious faith. For me this is specifically Christian Evangelical faith, which is the world that I grew up in, and the world I've always been at home in—until now.

To help those who are not familiar with this world, here's what it's like. (This is perhaps overly simplistic, but maybe not.) You live in two worlds: your "church" or "Christian" world, your "Sunday" world—where you can "be yourself" because you're surrounded by people who "get you." Then there's the world that you go out into on Monday—the world that is indifferent, or even hostile to, the world you are most comfortable in. You grow up knowing that you're different from most other people in what you believe about religious matters and that they don't get you because you don't see life the way they do. You feel a kind of distance from them because they are simply indifferent about your faith, but your faith is supposed to be everything to you. You are most comfortable when you're in your Christian world, and while you've managed to function rather normally and even somewhat comfortably in your non-Christian world, you're never quite fully "at home" when you emerge from your comfort zone into the "real world."

You function in your non-Christian world with a constant awareness that you're different—not entirely, but in that one area of religious adherence. While you learn to live and function somewhat normally and comfortably outside of your faith world, you experience a sense of guilt if you're not being overtly "Christian" when you're out there at your job, school, or wherever. You want to be a "good Christian," which means that you live with a sense of obligation to articulate your faith to nonbelievers because you've always believed that yours is the only true faith—the only faith that "guarantees" eternal life. So you've always been taught that's what you're supposed to do: "share" your faith. You might not be comfortable with the thought. Nevertheless, you believe it's true that no other faith tradition or belief system qualifies its adherents as recipients of that eternal bliss that you know you have in your back pocket. And, although you wouldn't admit it openly, you carry around with you that nagging thought that anyone who fails to accept/believe the Christian message is doomed to eternal damnation and separation from God.

Furthermore, if you had occasion to reach out to someone with the gospel message, but didn't, you felt that you had utterly failed in your Christian duty. This obligation is, in fact, so guilt-ridden that if you found yourself seated next to someone on an airplane, for example, it was to be considered a foreordained "divine appointment," and it was your Christian duty to present the gospel to that person. Because, after all, the stakes are the highest: Whether or not you chose to engage him or her with the "good news" (gospel) might very well determine that person's eternal destiny.

These are the kinds of thoughts I grew up with as a professing Christian. They are uncomfortable thoughts. They carried with them a sense of guilt and inadequacy, and they are in fact meant to do so. I would go so far as to claim that if you consider yourself an Evangelical Christian and you don't relate (even if only a little bit) to what I just described, you are in the minority of Evangelical Christians. I believe that this way of thinking is what Brian McLaren was criticizing when described the "shrunken gospel":

> Jesus does not prescribe hell to those who refuse to accept the message of justification by grace through faith, or those who are predestined for perdition, or those who don't profess acceptance of Jesus as their "personal savior . . ." Sadly, in too many quarters we reduce the scope of the gospel to the individual soul, framing it in a personalized format . . . This domesticated gospel will not rock any boats; it is a "shrinking gospel."[58]

---

58. Brian McLaren, *Everything Must Change: Jesus, Global Crises, and a Revolution of Hope* (Nashville, TN: Thomas Nelson, Inc., 2007), pages 208 and 244.

If you are genuinely convinced and comfortable with the idea that among all the world's religions, you alone hold the one and only true faith, then clearly the viewpoint presented in this book is not resonating with you. That's for you to decide. But one of the conclusions that can be drawn from my argument in this book is that it seems self-evidently egocentric to believe in a God who is so small-minded and conflicting as to create a humanity in whom he has deposited the miraculously amazing capacity to reason out of our own being; with the ability to intuitively know the difference between good and evil; to think lofty and profound thoughts; to design and create beauty; and yet, at the same time to be a God who disregards that reasoning, intuition, loftiness, and creativity as ultimately inconsequential in the larger scheme of eternity, unless one is an adherent or believer of one particular biblical faith. One could reasonably posit that such a God would be a pure enigma, an absolute contradiction.

So, once again: How does one go about grappling with that most important question: *What do I believe to be the absolute truth?* I have come to the conclusion that, for any thoughtful person, your current body of theological belief, no matter how strongly you adhere to it today, doesn't necessarily define your lifelong body of belief. One who is not easily persuaded to change his or her beliefs is, in some respect, fortunate. It's not a place of comfort to be shifting in one's most foundational beliefs. But on the other hand, since the ultimate question—*What is the absolute truth?*—is the most important of all questions, why shouldn't we at least take a reasonable stab at digging in and looking for answers, as far as we can within our obvious limitations?

Toward that end, as a professing Christian, I believe that as a starting point we must come face to face with the question "What do I believe?", which is obviously not the same question as *What is the absolute truth?* No matter how well-reasoned, no matter how seriously I pursue truth, in the end, what I believe is my subjective opinion. It is what I regard as truth based on the evidence that I choose to accept—but that obviously doesn't mean it's true. It is merely my own personal journey through trying to answer life's big questions. As I tried to explain above, there is—there must be—an ultimate truth that is true for all of humanity.

So let me start there: *What do I believe?* What is my personal "truth journey"? I've already written about my journey through youth and early adulthood, and as I pointed out, my journey really took a serious turn when I entered the world of academia. Up to that time, I had never questioned what I regarded as ultimate truth in the Christian world I had grown up in, until I came face to face with Judaism. After earning a master's degree in Hebrew and taking two years of graduate study in Hebrew Bible, in 1987 I started working at the Institute for Advanced Jewish Studies (as mentioned above), and in 1993 I took on the position as administrator of the Institute.

Over time I have become increasingly comfortable in the atmosphere of academia, working alongside Jews and Christians (both nominal and actively religious, but all serious academics). At the same time, I have continued living in my "Sunday Christian world," in which Judaism is seen as the "old" (obsolete) faith that was supplanted by the New Testament faith. In order to explore that world within the context of the larger sphere of religiously oriented observance, it will be helpful to look at a sketch of biblical history.

A brief sketch of biblical history

Within the world of Judaism, a world in which I've spent much of my professional adult life, I observe a vibrant religious community, a faith community, a community of believers who are committed to following their revealed biblical faith: the faith of the Hebrew Bible—what Christians call the Old Testament, a body of writing that we Christians (no less than observing Jews) fully regard as authoritative Scripture. The Old Testament constitutes the most important text for Jews, a community that has continued, since the giving of the law at Sinai, for some 3,500 years! Jews strive to observe and live by the truth of that revelation, to pin their eternal hope on the truth of that revelation. But as goes the human experience, life consists of ups and downs, successes and failures, hopes and dashed hopes. It was no different in ancient Israel than it is for us today. And so along came the prophets of Israel, who spoke out against human failure and preached hope to a religious community that had lost its way.

In the midst of all that, Jesus came on the scene and changed everything. The drama of what happened then—and in the few years following his lifetime—was unimaginable in human history. It was dramatic enough to split the timeline of history from BCE to CE. Jesus accomplished nothing short of redefining the big question I asked above: "What is truth?" Up until Jesus entered the scene, the "truth" was God's revelation to the Jewish nation, as transmitted and codified in scriptural form by the inspired writers of the Bible, end of story! No religiously adherent Jew would dare to allow the removal from or addition to that revelation. The Hebrew Bible, the Old Testament, represents the complete and authoritative divine revelation.

But, we Christians have the New Testament in addition to the Old—divine revelation continues where the Old Testament leaves off. The continuity is seamless, we claim. God's unfinished redemptive story finds completion in the New Testament. It's not as if Jesus and the New Testament writers were bringing a revelation that contradicted the Jewish Scriptures. Nor do we say that Jesus was adding a new or different category to revealed Scripture. In fact, we claim, Jesus was merely "drawing out" the true meaning of the Jewish Scriptures. He was bringing out the "hidden truths" of the texts— those truths that were implied or partially revealed but only now could be fully revealed and understood as being fulfilled in the person of Jesus, the incarnate God. It makes perfect sense to us, who (although not having the benefit of being beneficiaries of God's promises to the Jews, and therefore not recipients of God's grace up to that point) could now be included in God's family because of the grace offered through Jesus's self-sacrifice, which provided a way of salvation for all, not just Jews. Great news for us non-Jews because we're no longer without hope. But what about the Jews?

If in fact this new revelation about Jesus were for us Gentiles only, and the Jewish nation was left to continue living in the light of the completed revelation given to them at Sinai and through the prophets, all would make sense. If the salvation Jesus offered was not interpreted and expounded by New Testament writers in a way that delegitimized the efficacy of what had been—since the beginning of Judaism—the true and complete revealed word of God, that would have made good sense to the Jews. Not only that, it would also certainly have indicated to the Jewish world that God's desire to include all of humanity in His salvific plan was not limited to Jews alone, but was much broader than that—in fact, it would have indicated that God's generous reach extended to the whole world.

But that's not what happened. Rather than being presented as an expanded, revealed salvation scheme to include Gentiles, the gospel of Jesus became, in the mind of Jesus's followers, a revelation that *replaced* the old way, making it ineffective, obsolete, incomplete, and therefore useless as a self-contained, effectual redemptive plan.

Of course we Christians don't articulate this—or even see it—that way. We understand the new work of Jesus not as a replacement of the old faith, but as a "completion" or fulfillment of it. But here's where I claim we fail to grasp the spirit of the biblical message. When we say that the Old Testament revelation is incomplete or insufficient without the addition of the New, what we are literally saying is that every Jew who believes and faithfully follows his or her full and complete revelation—that is, every Jew who has believed in, practiced, and staked their eternal destiny on God's redemptive grace as presented in the Hebrew Scriptures—really does not have any hope of salvation after all. A boldly presumptuous statement? Perhaps. But is there any other way to interpret the Christian claim? In his excellent introduction to Rosemary Ruether's book *Faith and Fratricide,* Gregory Baum writes:

> As long as the Christian Church regards itself as the successor of Israel, as the new people of God substituted in the place of the old, and as long as the Church proclaims Jesus as the one mediator without whom there is no salvation, no theological space is left for other religions, and, in particular, no theological validity is left for the Jewish religion.[59]

* * *

---

59. Rosemary Ruether, *Faith and Fratricide: The Theological Roots of Anti-Semitism* (Eugene, OR: Wipf and Stock, 1996), page 5. For a clear and concise explanation of the problem of "replacement theology," see Rosemary Ruether's excellent summary in another of her books, *Disputed Questions: On Being a Christian* (Nashville, TN: Abingdon Press, 1982), pages 57–59.

With that as background, let me make some observations that follow from the view that sees the Old Testament revelation as incomplete without the New. First, a negative observation. In my experience, we Christians hopelessly fail to grasp the simple truth that virtually no practicing Jew (I say "virtually" to stress my point, even though there are of course exceptions) will come to a "redemptive knowledge" of Jesus as prescribed by the New Testament gospel message. To do so would be to deny his or her faith, to come to the point of believing that his or her revealed faith is insufficient, defunct, in vain. And here's my point: *As a non-Jew, professing belief in Jesus, I find indefensible and incomprehensible the notion that the world of Judaism is living without hope based on their collective denial of the need for an additional revelatory corpus beyond their own Scriptural tradition.*

Christian theology, especially Reformed Christianity, of course doesn't present such a hopeless picture. Rather, it generally presents itself as being respectful and even grateful for its Judaic origins. We like to talk about our "Judeo-Christian heritage," conferring on ourselves the idea that we're in sync, or on board, with God's unfolding plan for the ultimate salvation of people from every nationality. We like to think that we, the church, are the logical outworking, the next (and last) step in God's ongoing and unfolding plan to redeem His people. We are (generally) careful to avoid saying that the church replaces Judaism as God's chosen, but at the core, and without apology, we believe that to be the truth, since we can't avoid coming to that conclusion if we are honest with the textual (New Testament) evidence.

The "E" word

In the Christian milieu in which I grew up, we would never have used the term "replacement theology" to characterize our position in relation to those whom we understood to be "outside" of the sphere of God's good graces. Nor would a sensitive Evangelical Christian use that term today. Yet, that is exactly the right term to describe what we believed based on Paul's understanding of believers in Jesus as the "New Israel," or what Paul himself calls the "Israel of God" (Galatians 6:16).[60] Replacement theol-

---

60. Thomas Schreiner, "The Church as the New Israel" in *Studia Biblica* 13 (1983), pages 17–38.

ogy is a pejorative yet fully accurate way to characterize those who were formerly under God's blessing but no longer are. We are certainly careful not to use the term because it is pregnant with negative (although fully intended) meaning. In short, it was, and is, offensive.

But where do we get the idea of replacement theology? Clearly it comes from Paul's theology of "election." In my view, the doctrine of divine election is the single most destructive New Testament concept, on two levels: corporate and individual. On the corporate level, Paul is quite clear in declaring that the former way of Judaism is superseded by the Church. On the other hand, he is also quite clear in saying that individual Jews can no longer rely on their divinely revealed protocol for how to relate to God. On the individual level, the New Testament—especially Paul—is also clear that God chooses or predestines some among humanity whom He will save, which can only infer its opposite—that God *does not* choose or predestine others for salvation. Such a claim deserves some detailed explanation. What is so troubling about the Pauline theology of election? The famous Reformed theologian G. C. Berkouwer, himself fully committed to the idea of divine election, called it a "dangerous" doctrine. In the opening paragraph of his book on the subject, he wrote:

> When reflecting on the confession of the Christian Church regarding election, one must be well aware of the many dangers that surround this doctrine . . . These dangers are not merely theoretical; they touch upon the religious life as a whole. It has happened more than once that a misinterpretation of this doctrine has made its results felt for generations.[61]

So far so good, although notice right away that even Berkouwer's disclaimer (the likelihood of misinterpretation) shows that the idea, in and of itself, is open to problems. Yet, in his chapter, "Election and Arbitrariness," he tries to escape the pitfalls of that danger by arguing that God, because He is God, cannot be subject to the same standard of man's arbitrariness, because ". . . it is impossible to subject Him to a law above Himself to curb

---

61. G. C. Berkouwer, *Divine Election* (Grand Rapids, MI: Eerdmans Publishing, 1950), page 7.

His arbitrariness."[62] He goes on to say that ". . . arbitrariness is ruled out by the sovereignty of [God's] election."[63] The obvious question follows: Is it not the very definition of sovereignty that the one who is sovereign gets to make arbitrary decisions? Berkouwer and others see the idea of arbitrariness as simply "whimsical; despotic; tyrannical; capricious; unreasonable; unsupported" (Berkouwer's words), which is certainly the negative side of the definition. But arbitrariness is also defined as "subject to individual will or judgment without restriction; contingent solely upon one's discretion . . ."; "decided by a judge or arbiter rather than by a law or statute; having unlimited power; uncontrolled or unrestricted by law . . ." (again, Berkouwer's words).

Those meanings of arbitrariness simply cannot be understood in any other way except as a commitment to the idea of God's complete and unaffected sovereignty in election, and therefore, it can only follow that if God elects. He is arbitrary in that process, not out of "tyranny or capriciousness," but out of His discretion as the One who is "unrestricted by law." All of the theological complications aside, the real question that follows simply can't be escaped: What does the idea of election say about the fairness or unfairness of a God who makes His elections based on arbitrariness? In other words, if God's sovereignty assumes His right to be arbitrary—which, according the biblical evidence, it clearly does—why characterize the idea of arbitrariness as a negative quality? Why try to "protect" God from the accusation of unfairness, which is in fact exactly what Berkouwer does? In his chapter "Election and Arbitrariness," he goes to great lengths to deny the claim of God's arbitrariness by calling it by several other names: "absolute power"; "royal authority"; "radical independence"; "not subject to a higher law"; a "law to himself"; "mystery of the depth of Christ's love"; "divine purpose"; God's "free act," etc.[64]

---

62. Ibid, page 55.

63. Ibid, page 76.

64. G. C. Berkouwer, *Divine Election* (Grand Rapids, MI: Eerdmans Publishing, 1950), pages 53–97.

Again, why go through the effort to protect God from the negative connotations of arbitrariness, if that is exactly an accurate and fair characterization? I will argue that the claim that God chooses whom to save—typical of theologians like Berkouwer, Calvin, and virtually all proponents of election—is an impossible, indefensible, and even nonsensical position. It is, indeed, as John Calvin put it (although without the justification in which he so carefully crafted it) a "horrible decree."

Calvinism and the doctrine of election

Simply defined, divine election is the idea that God, within His divine right, predetermines and chooses whom He will save. The most comprehensive biblical text on the doctrine, Romans 8:20, uses four words to lay out the idea that God chooses those He predetermines to save: "Those whom He *predestined* He also *called*; and those whom He called He also *justified*; and those whom He justified he also *glorified*." To be sure, the reality of divine election is clearly defensible from this and other Scriptures, for example, in texts like Acts 13:48 where, after hearing Paul preach it is noted that "as many as were *appointed* to eternal life believed." As I'll show below, Paul is explicit in his defense of election.

Now, there are all kinds of biblically supportable caveats to that simple definition above that proponents of election would cite, to soften the blow of the inescapable implication. For example, Christ died for the sins of the *whole* world (*"He is the atoning sacrifice . . . not only for our sins, but for the sins of the whole world."* 1 John 2:2); God's invitation to His grace is open to all who put their faith in Him (*"Everyone who calls on the name of the Lord will be saved."* Rom 10:13). In the end, however, it can't be both ways; one can't propose a God who is totally free in election and who therefore chooses to save some people and not save others, but who also extends a *legitimate* offer of salvation to everyone. It is an impossible contradiction. As Rudolf Otto noted:

> It is perhaps precisely the "rationalist" who feels most directly that with the idea of predestination we are standing on downright non-rational ground. Nothing remains so alien to the rationalist as

this doctrine. And from his point of view, he is quite right; from the stand point of the rational, this notion of predestination is a sheer absurdity, an absolute offence. Let him acquiesce in all the paradoxes of the Trinity and Christology, predestination will yet remain perpetually to confront him as a stumbling-block.[65]

A good Calvinist would argue that God can do what seems impossible to man, or that God, because He is God, cannot be judged by man as to his actions. But that's not an answer because (1) It defies the rules of logic, which even a Calvinist would agree originate from God; and (2) It puts God in a position to do something that everyone (including a staunch Calvinist) would agree is against His own nature: contradict Himself.

Unresolved questions

So many obvious questions arise from the point of view that sees divine election as a foundational attribute of God's will—questions about God's justice and mercy, questions about His sense of fairness, on and on. The usual "safe" response is that we don't question God because the Bible tells us that "his ways are higher than ours" (Isaiah 55:8–9), or as Berkouwer put it, "God is above arbitrariness." But it's very interesting that Paul himself felt the need to defend God's unchallenged right to choose some but not others in his rather lengthy defense in Romans 9:

> You will say to me then, "Why does He still find fault? For who resists His will?" On the contrary, who are you, O man, who answers back to God? The thing molded will not say to the molder, "Why did you make me like this," will it? Or does not the potter have a right over the clay, to make from the same lump one vessel for honorable use and another for common use? What if God, although willing to demonstrate His wrath and to make His power known, endured with much patience vessels of wrath prepared for destruction? And *He did so* to make known the riches of His glory

---

65. Rudolf Otto, *The Idea of the Holy: An Inquiry into the Non-rational Factor in the Idea of the Divine and its Relation to the Rational* (New York: Oxford University Press, 1958), page 86.

upon vessels of mercy, which He prepared beforehand for glory. (Romans 9:19–23)

My point is this: If the biblical idea of divine election is something that we should accept without question, why did Paul himself make the effort to present such a detailed defense? Should not Paul (like reformed Evangelical defenders of the doctrine) have been satisfied to give the patent answer, "Don't question God," and leave it at that? Interestingly, in the text above, Paul starts out saying just that: Don't question God (v. 20). But then he goes on to give a defense on God's behalf (v. 22–23), an answer that actually implicates God as one who sets up some people to fail: ". . . enduring with patience vessels of wrath *prepared for destruction . . . beforehand*." Paul here leaves no doubt that it is God's predetermination alone—not people's behavior—that determines His electing activity.

Mystery Versus Contradiction: More Questions Than Answers

The idea of biblical mystery is a comfortable and safe place for proponents of election to turn to. Virtually any seeming contradiction in God's character can be easily dismissed by the claim that it's a deep and hidden mystery that only God can understand. But as Roger Olson explains:

> We must point out the difference between mystery and contradiction; the former is something that cannot be fully explained to or comprehended by the human mind whereas the latter is sheer nonsense—two concepts that cancel each other out and together make an absurdity. Christian theology should never rest comfortably with the latter [contradiction] whereas the former [mystery] is always going to be present in human talk of God.[66]

The reason that contradiction as a divine prerogative can be so easily dismissed is because the mystery of God is a category that is outside of hu-

---

66. Roger E. Olson, *Against Calvinism: Rescuing God's Reputation from Radical Reformed Theology* (Grand Rapids, MI: Zondervan Publishing, 2011), page 105.

mans' capacity to understand, and therefore to question as to its intent. So
every seemingly contradictory act of God can be placed in the category of
mystery, thereby relieving people of the obligation to explain or apologize
for God's seemingly inconsistent and uncharacteristic actions. Simply put,
declaring God's questionable acts as "mysteries" puts them off limits to
those who would dig deeper into the dilemma presented by the obvious
contradiction.

The argument about biblical mystery goes something like this: Since God's
ways are far beyond our understanding, we can never hope to probe into
the eternal mind. So while we should study and grapple with biblical ideas,
there comes a point when we must stop questioning things that we don't
understand; rather, we should realize that (as Paul tells us in 1 Corinthians
13:12), "We see dimly now, but one day we will see clearly" enough to
make sense of what doesn't make sense now. But again, as Olson points out
(see quotation above), this thinking confuses the two very different concepts—mystery versus contradiction. A mystery can be a beautiful thing.
As Harvey Cox put it: "A mystery is not something anyone solves. It is
something we live with, and people find that this mystery touches them in
different ways."[67] When something is mysterious, it is intriguing; it arrests
our mind and heart and opens our eyes to conjure images and ideas that we
wouldn't otherwise grasp, images that can enrich the soul because they are
far beyond our capacity to absorb through physical sight.

In his book, *Das Heilige* (translated into English as *The Idea of the Holy*),[68]
Rudolf Otto described mystery as the primal experience of awe or wonder,
what Mircea Eliade calls the irrational aspect of the religious experience.[69]
The point, of course, is that although it is irrational, it is no less real. Otto
used the phrase *mysterium tremendum* to describe the emotion. The problem with Calvinism is that it resorts to the argument of mystery to mitigate
the obvious contradiction of a God who appears to perform both good and

67. Harvey Cox, *The Future of Faith:* (New York: HarperCollins, 2009), page 24.

68. Rudolf Otto, *The Idea of the Holy: An Inquiry into the Non-rational Factor in the Idea of the Divine and its Relation to the Rational* (New York: Oxford University Press, 1958).

69. Mircea Eliade, *The Sacred and the Profane: The Nature of Religion* (New York: Harcourt, Brace &
Company, 1959).

evil deeds by shrouding those deeds in some sort of inexplicable ethical scheme that is beyond challenge, a scheme that applies to God and no one else because, after all, God's sense of rationality and morality are not subject to humanity's approval. But by any definition, a good being, whether divine or human, cannot also be evil. Nor can our sense of "evil" be redefined to mean one thing for us and something completely different (and in fact opposite) for God. In short, to define an apparent contradiction as mystery is nonsensical. Contradiction is actually the opposite of mystery. James Daane explains the difference:

> . . . I will argue that high Calvinism falls into contradictions; it cannot be made intelligible—and Christianity should be intelligible. By 'intelligible' I do not mean philosophically rational; I mean capable of being understood. A sheer contradiction is a sure sign of error; even most Calvinists agree about that. The greatest contradiction is that God is confessed as perfectly good while at the same time described as the author of sin and evil . . . Not all Calvinists admit that their theology makes God the author of sin and evil; many deny that. But . . . it is a good and necessary consequence of what else they say about God.[70]

Can one honestly imagine the idea of divine election as a beautiful mystery? Only by defying every possible meaning of the word "goodness" can one reach the conclusion that God in His infinite goodness chooses one person for eternal bliss but chooses another person as (in Paul's words) "a vessel prepared for destruction" (Rom. 9:22). By any measure of rationality, can anyone believe that a perfectly benevolent God is also the author of sin and evil? How is it possible to come to a place of satisfaction and resolve about the character of a good God in light of the idea that He is, at the same time, a God who punishes arbitrarily?

But that's what the Bible says, isn't it? Note Paul's indignation when he asks: "Who are you to question God?" (Rom. 9:19). So where does that

---

70. James Daane, *The Freedom of God: A Study in Election and Pulpit* (Grand Rapids, MI: Eerdmans Publishing, 2015), page 25.

leave those of us who profess Christianity but can't accept the conclusion that seems to be clearly presented by Paul and the defenders of his theology? To illustrate dramatically what proponents of divine election believe, I note examples from two of the most popular proponents of the doctrine of divine election, one early and one modern:

John Calvin:

> Those whom God passes over he condemns, and this he does for no other reason than that he wills to exclude them from the inheritance which he predestines for his own children.[71]

This statement is what Calvin himself called "God's horrible decree." Such a statement by Calvin seems remarkably inflammatory and extremely troubling as representing God's character. Why? Because it could only be made by someone who has experienced the grace of God to the extent where he believes it only because he is on the *right side* of the extended grace (i.e., he's one of "God's own children"). Think about it. No one who is on the outside of that grace would dare to make such an argument, as that would constitute his or her affirmation of self-condemnation to eternal suffering. Only a fully committed hyper-Calvinist could write such inflammatory and chilling statements as John Piper has written: "It's right for God to slaughter women and children anytime he pleases. God gives life, and he takes life. Everybody who dies, dies because God wills that they die."[72]

Or as Piper writes elsewhere:

> God's heart is capable of complex combinations of emotions infinitely more remarkable than ours. He may well be capable of lamenting over something he chose to bring about. And God may be capable of looking back on the very act of bringing something

71. John Calvin, *Institutes of the Christian Religion* (various editions).

72. John Piper, "What Made it Okay for God to Kill Women and Children in the Old Testament?" https://www.desiringgod.org/interviews/what-made-it-okay-for-god-to-kill-women-and-children-in-the-old-testament about and lamenting that act in one regard, while affirming it as best in another regard.[73]

The level of mental gymnastics required to make sense of such a convoluted proposition is astounding. It would actually be ludicrous if it weren't so harmfully malicious. Is Piper actually saying that God is "emotionally" (Piper's word) torn to the point that He acts in one way only to regret ("lament") his decision to act in that way, while at the same time affirming that He did the right thing after all? Such a contradictory characterization makes God out to be wishy-washy and indecisive in His temperament. And by way of explanation of that statement, Piper goes on to cite the example of spanking a disobedient child as a "necessary and wise way of dealing with the situation." Really? To characterize God's eternal damnation of individuals in a lake of fire as a loving act comparable to a parent's spanking of a child is so callous as to defy explanation.

In the texts cited above, it is God's prerogative alone that determines the fate of every individual. Nothing is left to human behavior (whether good or bad), and nothing is left to human choice. Notice the incendiary language attributed to God's behavior: "he passes over and condemns for *no other reason* than that he wills to do so" . . . ". . . he does so ". . . anytime he pleases."

I have to agree with Roger Olson, who candidly but justifiably responds to such statements by Calvinists:

> . . . Someone needs finally to stand up and . . . firmly say 'No!' to egregious statements about God's sovereignty often made by Calvinists. Taken to their logical conclusion, that even hell and all who will suffer there eternally are foreordained by God, God is thereby rendered morally ambiguous at best and a moral monster

---

73. John Piper, "God Does Not Repent Like a Man" https://www.desiringgod.org/articles/god-does-not-repent-like-a-man)

at worst . . . This kind of Calvinism . . . makes it difficult to see the difference between God and the devil . . .[74]

The Calvinist arguments for this extreme brand of election are supported by a phenomenon called "decretal theology," and specifically the idea of God's "single decree" that God's eternal decrees stand for all time and operate regardless of historical eventualities. Decretal theology is the negative side of the biblical idea of God's unchangeableness. God is not free to act outside of his decretal pronouncements. The consequence of the single decree is that it is unaffected by world history. As James Daane explains it:

> Nothing in the world and its history determines, affects, or conditions God's decree. Nothing in the decree, then, is of the nature of a free divine response to the realities of history. Thus, Election is not God's free response to the plight of sinful fallen men. Mercy and grace are not God's free response . . . compassion is not a free response of God to the sufferings and misery of the sinner . . . In sum, God is not free to act in history outside of his own decree, or he would be working against himself. This ignores the freedom of God to "go historical" = to move creatively, in time, toward creation and redemption.[75]

Aside from the fact that this theology presents God as weak and unable to act outside of His own preordained guidelines, even worse, the implication of such a theology is that it places God outside of, and not related to, the world. It claims that God is the ultimate "cause" of sin (since He decreed it), but He's not the author of sin. I'm not sure how that contradiction can be explained. By some kind of twisted logic, "causing" an action is not the same thing as "authoring" that action. Again, a Calvinist can only declare that it's not really a contradiction, it only seems like one. We don't get it because we're not God—we have limited and finite comprehension. As James Daane put it: "In short, whenever decretal theology is matched with his-

74. Roger Olson, *Against Calvinism: Rescuing God's Reputation from Radical Reformed Theology* (Grand Rapids, MI: Zondervan Publishing, 2011), page 23.

75. James Daane, *The Freedom of God: The Freedom of God: A Study of Election and Pulpit* (Grand Rapids, MI: Eerdmans Publishing, 2015), pages 61–62.

tory, it appears tragically unrelated to the facts of life."[76] It is my view that Calvinism, while it is no doubt sincere in its determination to characterize God rightly, grossly misunderstands those core truths concerning what it *must mean* to be God, truths that, if tainted by contradictory characteristics, compromise His being beyond recognition as God.

Such a convolution of ideas regarding the character of God leads one to ask the question: What is the core truth about God, the simple but profound truth, uncomplicated by the theologically absurd and contradictory argument above? Very simply, we want to know the truth that above all else, God, if He *is* God in the universally understood sense of what that means, must absolutely be good, meaning that He must be merciful, loving, and kind above all else. Let's now dig a little deeper into the character of that loving and merciful God. No discussion about a good God can be complete without saying something about His quality of truthfulness.

The big question: What is the truth?

Trying to navigate through the discussion above only leaves one baffled and more confused than ever. It makes one long for a straightforward and uncomplicated truth about God and theology that transcends all other truths. I think it's fair to say that Pilate's famous question recorded in John 18:38—"What is truth?"—is really the big question, certainly the biggest question asked of Jesus in the Bible. And in fact, the answer was apparently so self-evident to Pilate that he answers it himself: "I find no fault in him." In other words, "The truth is here standing before you . . ."

I love what Paul Tillich writes about Pilate's question: "For those among us for whom Pilate's question is alive . . . in the depth of every serious doubt and very despair of truth, the passion for truth is still at work."[77] Tillich goes on to state that when one is serious about the question of truth, he is

76. James Daane, *The Freedom of God: A Study of Election and Pulpit* (Grand Rapids, MI: Eerdmans Publishing, 2015), pages 82–83.

77. Paul Tillich, *The New Being*. New York: Charles Scribner's Sons, 1955, page 67.

already on his way to liberation, so that even while in the midst of despair, he has "already started to emerge from it."

It seems clear that, taking the Bible as a whole—both the Old and New Testaments—there appears to be a major contradiction in the claims that Scripture makes in answer to the question, What is the truth? But for the sake of clarity, let's narrow the question to "What is the truth about humankind's destiny?" What does it take for humans to be able to reach God? (This is, after all, *the* big question.) If you're following my argument up to this point, you might not be surprised that I would propose two answers: one in the Old Testament and the other in the New Testament.

The Old Testament answer is clear, and is perhaps most succinctly summarized by the prophet Micah in his answer to the question: "How shall I come before the Lord?" The prophet's answer (Micah 6:8): "He [the Lord] has told you, O man, what is good; and what does the Lord require of you but *to do justice and to love kindness, and to walk humbly with your God.*" Can a statement of God's intent be any clearer? What does it take to be accepted by God? To live in a way that extends kindness and acts toward others with humility.

Turning to Isaiah, we see clear evidence of God's salvation of Israel: "Thus says the Lord, he who created you O Jacob, he who formed you O Israel: Fear not for I have *redeemed* you, I have called you by name, you are mine" (Isa. 43:1). Can anything be clearer in affirming God's salvation (redemption) of Israel? He goes on in v. 3 to say: "For I am the Lord your God, the Holy One of Israel, *your Savior.*" And in v. 11: "I am the Lord, and *besides me there is no savior.*" Isaiah continues in the following chapters to make it perfectly clear that Israel is assured of God's salvation.

Turning to the New Testament, we find that a person's destiny is governed not by how he or she lives or by God's simple calling out of a nation (as in the Isaiah texts), but by simple affirmative response to Jesus's offer of saving grace. What emerges when we look at God's way of salvation in the Old and New Testaments is a situation where we see two different coherent self-contained paths of humanity's relation to God. The idea of "progressive revelation," which is nothing more than a respectable and polite way to characterize replacement theology, fails to grasp the special character of God's multifaceted redemptive plan. Replacement theology (or progressive revelation) would have us understand that there is only one way to God, universally across the spectrum of humanity, that His means of offering grace to humanity before the advent of Christ was never intended to apply with any permanence. It implies that God cannot present two different means of or roads to salvation for two different groups of people. The obvious question is "Why not?" I'll say more about this question below, when we dig a little deeper into Paul's theology of election in Romans.

Faith, Sovereignty, And Free Will

Gregory Boyd's argument in his book, *The God of the Possible*[78] presents more of a challenge for me because his theological position, while attractive to me personally, is widely unaccepted in my Evangelical circle. Boyd is clearly a believer in open theism—which defines the sovereignty of God as meaning that God foreknows and is sovereign over *all that He purposes to know and control,* and that He selectively decides not to know every detail of life. The basic premise behind open theism is that, since God is the God of all creation, He is the God of possibilities, as well as eternally settled realities.

Like others who have thought through these issues, I have always struggled with the apparent disconnect between the two biblical truths of God's sovereignty and man's free will. And I am convinced that both doctrines are 100 percent biblical. Why? Because I could not have faith in a God who I did not believe was sovereign. And I could not trust a God who claims to have given me a free will that is not literally, completely, genuinely *free.* In other words, what could only be called "controlled free will" is a nonsensical self-contradiction—it's simply impossible for God to give me something that He didn't really give me. This leaves me with only two

---

78. Gregory Boyd, *The God of the Possible: A Biblical Introduction to the Open View of God* (Ada, MI: Baker Books, 2000).

alternatives with regard to reconciling the idea of God's sovereignty, both unworkable.

Option #1: Sovereignty and mystery are both valid and work together

The first option is to do what most Evangelical Christians do: declare ignorance. Not only do they declare ignorance, but they claim in fact that ignorance is the only right and commendable response to the unexplainable mystery. That is, they try to understand both human free will and divine sovereignty as true biblical dogmas, conceding any possibility of reconciling them. And they adopt the position of the Apostle Paul and acknowledge that God is sovereign over everything, including decisions that I will make throughout my life; and at the same time to believe that my actions have real meaning, that I am completely free and responsible for my decisions and deeds.

This is, in fact, the position taken by the Evangelical community. In that case, we have to concede (and find satisfaction in the idea) that we can make no logical sense out of the concept of God's sovereignty and what that means, since that is the inescapable conclusion of such a proposition. And that is exactly where Paul's theology leaves us. For I know without a doubt what my human free will means, there's no ambiguity, I am completely qualified to know, I am human after all, so I exercise it. Free will means that I have complete control over my own decisions and actions—when I come to a crossroads, I choose to go either left or right. Sound reasoning can only reject the idea that freedom of the will means (as some would claim) freedom to choose what God has predetermined one would choose. That, of course, is a nonsensical idea—it is simply not free will. So my understanding of what it means to have free choice is clear. I encounter it every day. God's sovereignty, on the other hand, is a foreign idea to me. Since I am on such a vastly different plane from God (He as the eternal, uncreated being; I as a mortal, created being), how can I truly understand the depths of the meaning of the idea of God's sovereignty? But the fact that I'm not capable of understanding God's sovereignty is not cause for me to reject the reality of His sovereignty while claiming only a partial

PART THREE: Journey Toward Faith

understanding of what it means. This option, of course, leaves us where we started—in an unresolvable dilemma.

Option #2: Sovereignty of God or mystery

The second option, which for me is unthinkable, is to accept one or the other doctrine as true and the other one as false, since two opposing and opposite propositions cannot both be true. Now, some might argue that two opposing notions can indeed be true. For example, H_2O can be a liquid or a solid, but it never ceases to be H_2O. But arguments like that don't hold water (pun intended) because the solid form of water (ice) is not its natural state but is conditioned by an outside influence (temperature). To argue this option of accepting one theological truth to the exclusion of the other, I would have no alternative but to deny God's sovereignty, since I cannot deny the absolute truth of my own free will. But as I said, that is unthinkable. It is clear to me that God, if He *is* God, must be sovereign. So where does that leave me?

A third option: purposeful sovereignty

The only way I can reconcile both truths (the truths of God's sovereignty and human free will) is to embrace God as sovereign and yet at the same time to accept my ignorance of all that divine sovereignty implies. And so perhaps the only reasonable conclusion I can draw (and I have not to this point settled the matter in my own mind, but I can find a level of satisfaction with it at least for now) is to take Boyd's position: that *God is sovereign over all that He purposes to be sovereign over.* All of life illustrates, and to some degree (although not fully) supports this notion. As a father, I can exercise *complete* sovereignty over the affairs of my children when they are under my care, *as long as they remain under my care.* I can dictate, one 100 percent, what they are and are not allowed to do, where they are and are not allowed to go, if I so choose.

But even as I exercise "complete" sovereignty over the areas of their life *that I choose to control*, I can give them "complete" freedom to make some fully independent choices—to play now and do homework later if that's their wish; what books to read, which friends to play with, even what kind of trouble to bring upon themselves—*all the while not knowing how they will choose, because I have come to know their character.* As parents, at times we even give our children freedom to choose something that can cause them harm. But the point is that unless we bring up our children in a protective bubble that will ensure freedom from harm (which in any case we can't do), we can never be sure that we're in complete control of their lives. So we *choose* not to exercise complete foreknowledge of what *might* occur in their lives as a result of their independent choices. This doesn't make us any less sovereign over their lives. Granted, the parent-child relationship obviously cannot fully carry the weight of serving as an adequate example of God's sovereignty over His creation. But the illustration is helpful in at least pointing out the possibility that God's allowing us freedom to make choices that might hurt us doesn't nullify the truth that He cares for His creation (as a loving father) or that He is ultimately in sovereign control.

In his book *The Faith and Modern Man*, Romano Guardini writes that: "God decreed that man do the good, and was therefore obliged to make him free, for the good which is fulfilled in action requires freedom . . ."[79] He goes on to state that the greatness of God's sovereignty reveals itself in this: "He willed to be Lord over free man, not over slaves or mere tools. And when he so willed, he accepted all that this decision implies . . . For God to interfere with the consequences would be to rob freedom of all seriousness."[80] I wonder what it is about the disposition or thought process that causes some committed Christians to be more confident in, or more devoted to, a God who would micromanage all our affairs and decisions—or have foreknowledge of everything about our future—rather than a God who gives us freedom to have complete sovereignty over some of our own affairs, even while not foreknowing which way we will choose.

I'm a parent of adult children. When they were young, it was clear to me that they trusted me—and even loved and respected me to a greater extent—when I gave them general guidelines (depending on their level

---

79. Romano Guardini, *The Faith and Modern Man* (New York: Pantheon Books, 1952), page 49.

80. Ibid, page 50.

of maturity and responsibility of course) to keep them safe and prosperous, but I also gave them the freedom to make their own choices at certain stages in their lives, even if I suspected that those choices might cause them harm. Rather than keep them in a protective bubble (which, again, I couldn't do anyway), perhaps it is a greater display of guiding love for parents to help their children by walking along with them as they work to resolve the painful situation or mistake that they created for themselves—in other words, to come to their aid as a resourceful and loving parent, who can come alongside them and help them resolve problems and correct mistakes, rather than guarantee that they never get into trouble or make mistakes.

Incidentally, as a father of children who are now adults, I've come to the conclusion that this sort of parenting style is not without both its risks and its great rewards. I know many families in my Evangelical circle in which parents have virtually micromanaged the development of thought processes of their children. Many, if not most, of these children have now grown to adulthood retaining the foundational thinking of their parents that has been funneled through their views on the biblical text, but some have not. I was that kind of parent for a good part of my children's upbringing. As secure and gratifying as that can be for a parent, as my own thinking evolved from blind biblical faith to a posture of questioning foundational beliefs, I felt it important and comfortable to be open and honest with my children about my evolving views. How that posture has served them and will serve them later in life remains to be seen.

In any case, what if any conclusion can be drawn from the view of God as more "open" in His sovereignty? Perhaps it is this—that an innovative God, a God who genuinely *reacts* to my failures and improvises His plans for me based on my failures, always perfectly and always for my best good, is certainly, for me, a God who is more interactive, more loving, more resourceful, and indeed more honest, than a God who feigns to give me free will while knowing all the time that He has foreordained and foreknown all my steps throughout eternity.

A few years I embarked upon a study through the Bible in an attempt to discover the biblical evidence on this question of free will. (I'm well familiar with what Scripture says about God's sovereignty—especially texts such as Psalm 139 and Romans 8—and I have a fairly robust understanding of what the Bible says about that aspect of His character.) But in my study I noted Scriptures that have to do with the following categories of God relating to man:

God *giving us choices*
    (as opposed to foreordaining all our choices)

God *asking us questions* to which he expects an answer
    (as opposed to him knowing all our responses beforehand)

God *repenting* or being sorry for an action He had taken
    (contrary to our common assumption that He cannot repent as man repents)

God changing His mind in response to man's intercession
    (contrary to our assumption that God's mind is unchangeable)

God *remembering* what He had said, and responding
    (contrary to our common assumption that God doesn't forget)

God *testing* man to see what he would do
    (as opposed to his pre-determination of man's responses)

God *being sure* about something
    (implying the possibility of His being unsure about some things)

And finally, God's sovereignty and man's free will working together.
    (a problem that is seemingly irreconcilable)

These types of questions about God—questions having to do with allowing choices, responding, remembering, testing, etc.—are questions that we instinctively relate only to human activity, never to divine operation. We do this because we find abhorrent the idea that God could ever be conflicted in His thinking and acting. So these types of questions intuitively seem like disrespectful or dangerous questions for us to entertain in relation to God. But why should that be so? If we are created in God's image, does it not follow that we (to a certain extent) reason and question as God's image bearers? I would argue that we shouldn't shy away from looking into these ideas about God—they are in the Bible. And we need to explore them as the serious questions that they are, questions that require much more than a cursory dismissal based on our preconceived notions of what God "must be like." To be honest in our reading of Scripture, we can't pick and choose what texts are to be read as truth versus fiction, factual, exaggeration, or hyperbole. The nature of the texts themselves determines how they are meant to be read.[81]

Having gone through the Torah (Genesis-Deuteronomy) I marked no fewer than 50 such texts. My purpose was simply to let the Bible speak for itself, to gain a truer understanding of God's responsiveness in relation to His dealings with humanity; and especially, to answer two questions. First, does God really mean what He says when He makes statements in the context of the categories listed above? Second, does the Bible teach (genuinely, that is, without us reading our preconceptions into the text) the principal of people's free will? In other words, is God being honest when He says that we have a free will to make choices, or is He saying something that He doesn't really mean, or is He speaking cryptically, so that in the mind of God, free will doesn't really, or literally, mean "free will"? In the end, I can find no justification for viewing these biblical texts in any other way but at face value. The only honest conclusion that can be drawn from such an exercise is that God *does* give us genuine choices. He *does* ask questions for which He seeks genuine answers. And when He "tests" people, He *is*

---

81. There is a whole other area of biblical genre that I won't address here, except to point out that, in general, Evangelicals have traditionally been reluctant to treat biblical text as anything but literal, thus ignoring the clear difference between what is to be read as literal truth and what is to be understood as nonliteral. But Evangelical Bible interpreters tend to be inconsistent in following that strict guideline of reading when it comes to texts that portray God as conflicted or questioning, as in the above examples.

giving genuine opportunity for them to respond—to succeed or fail as they choose.

Free choice and its consequences

Another argument for the possibility that God might not have foreordained all human actions is the very nature of His covenant with humans—that it is conditional, based on the covenantal formula "if . . .then . . .," which not only implies but logically demands that our actions and decisions in response to God are up to us and, therefore, are not settled in God's mind. Over and over again, especially in Deuteronomy, God is constantly laying out a clear choice for the Israelites—put simply, either obey and prosper or rebel and suffer the consequences. Although the Bible is unambiguous (for example in Deut. 31:16) in saying that God does *foresee* Israel's rebellion (again, in the same way that I, as a father, can "foresee" consequences of bad behavior in my children), it does not necessarily follow that he does not present them with a real choice. For example, in Deuteronomy 7:12, God says: "If you *hear* these ordinances, and *observe* them and *perform* them, the Lord your God will maintain with you the covenant loyalty that he swore to your ancestors . . ." Even more compelling is Deuteronomy 8:2, where God says: "Remember the long way that the Lord your God has led you to these forty years in the wilderness, in order to humble you, *to test* you, *to know* what was in your heart, *whether or not you would keep* His commandments." The language is crystal clear. Does God not really mean what he says? Why would He test their hearts *"to know whether or not"* they would keep his commandments if He already knew whether they would or wouldn't?

Perhaps the strongest text showing what seems to be a clear indication of the conditional nature of God's dealings with His people is Jeremiah 18—the parable of the potter and the clay vessel. At God's instruction, Jeremiah goes to the potter's house and observes him making a clay vessel, but when the vessel is not coming out to the potter's satisfaction, he starts over, reworking the clay again (Jeremiah 18:5–10). At this point the word of the Lord comes to Jeremiah:

O house of Israel, can I not do with you as this potter has done? Behold, like the clay in the potter's hand, so are you in my hand, O house of Israel. If at any time I declare concerning a nation or a kingdom that I will pluck up and break down and destroy it, *and if that nation, concerning which I have spoken, turns from its evil, I will relent of the disaster that I intended to do to it. And if at any time I declare concerning a nation or a kingdom that I will build and plant it, and if it does evil in my sight not listening to my voice, then I will relent of the good that I had intended to do to it* (italics added).

God then instructs Jeremiah to warn the Israelites to "turn from your evil way, amend your ways and deeds," the clear implication being that He is giving them a chance to turn God's hand away from the devastation He is about to bring on them. The point of the parable is clear—to show that Israel's rebellion or turning to God is *not* predetermined. God's response depends on yet-to-be-determined behavior.

How the doctrine of election derailed my ordination

As I was progressing toward ordination in my denomination up until two years ago, I was thinking more and more about the matter of election, since my espousal of that doctrine would have been a condition of my ordination. During that time, I wrote a lengthy letter to a close friend who happens to sit on the ordination committee, but I never sent the letter, for a variety of reasons. As it turned out, I stepped out of the ordination process because I couldn't reconcile my doubts with the requirements of the ordaining body. Here is my letter . . . I present it exactly as I composed it, both because it was my gut-level response at the time and because it still represents my rationale, as it did when I wrote it:

Dear _____,

As you know, this issue of election has been and continues to be a real problem for me. There isn't another issue of biblical thought that troubles me more than this, and obviously it has come to the foreground the closer I get to ordination.

I've spent the last month or so poring through several texts of both OT and NT, primarily Isaiah, Jeremiah, John, Romans, and Ephesians, from the point of view of what the Bible has to say about the question of God's universal call to salvation versus His exclusive call to the elect, and I have come no closer to resolving the question in my own mind. In fact, I'm more troubled than ever.

Using Paul's argument in Rom. 9–11 I'll try to lay out what I see as the central point in the issue of election, which continues to be an unresolved problem for me. Paul's presentation in Rom. 9–11, taken as a unit, is a coherent argument, and therefore I think it is the text that best shows both sides of the problem.

On one side of his argument, Paul is clear that God, in His mercy and love for his creation, has extended an offer for all people to hear his call and believe on him:

> Romans 10:4 Christ is the end of the law for righteousness *to everyone who believes.*

> 10:9 If you confess with your mouth that Jesus is Lord and believe in your heart that God raised Him from the dead you will be saved.

> 10:11 Everyone who believes in Him will not be put to shame.

> 10:12 He bestows His riches on all who call on Him.

> 10:16 But they have not all obeyed the gospel; for Isaiah says "Lord who has believed our report?" So faith comes from hearing, and hearing through the word of Christ.

> 10:21 Of Israel He says "All day long I have held out my hands to a disobedient and contrary people."

Yet, Paul is also clear, in this same argument, in saying the opposite—that God is merciful and loving *to those He has called out to save*:

9:12 So that God's purpose in election might continue, not because of works but because of him who calls, she was told . . . "Jacob I loved, but Esau I hated."

9:15 I will have mercy on whom I have mercy, compassion on whom I have compassion . . .

9:18 So then He has mercy on whomever He wills, and He hardens whomever He wills."

11:1–4 Has God rejected his people? By no means . . . I have kept for myself 7,000 men who have not bowed the knee to Baal.

11:25 A partial hardening has come upon Israel until the fullness of the Gentiles has come in. And in this way all Israel will be saved.

Romans 9:19–22 seems to be the center of Paul's argument. Paul himself seems to have realized the tension in what he was writing, because he poses a question that would certainly have occurred to his readers after his rather dramatic reminder of God's statement in Malachi 1:2: "I have loved Jacob, but Esau I have hated." Speaking on behalf of his readers, Paul asks the question: "You will say then, Why does he still find fault?"

I see this as the central crux of Paul's teaching on election—he's working through an answer to his own question—the question is really this. If God has prepared vessels of wrath for destruction (v. 22), and since those vessels are passive in becoming those vessels that they were created to be (v. 21), why then does He find fault with those vessels?

This is where Paul's teaching becomes incomprehensible to me. He is presenting an argument for which he doesn't draw a satisfying or reasonable conclusion. Verse 22 is crucial in his argument:

1. God prepared beforehand vessels of wrath for destruction.

   [but also]

2. God prepared beforehand vessels of mercy for glory.

[yet]

3. He endured with patience those vessels of wrath in order to make known his riches to the vessels of glory.

His response to the dilemma is v. 20 "Who are you to answer back to God? Doesn't the potter have the right over the clay . . ."

The answer of course is that He does. The potter can do whatever he desires to do with the clay. But that answers only one side of the question—it answers the question "Is God, the creator, justified in doing whatever He wants?" Of course He is. But Paul's answer doesn't speak to the real question that would have been on the minds of his readers—"Why then does God find fault?" One can't help but respond, "It seems so unfair!" Paul is saying, in no uncertain terms, that the Creator can rightfully put it in the heart of His subjects to reject Him, and punish them for that rejection. In other words, Paul doesn't answer his own question ("Why does He still find fault?"), because there is no answer. Rather, Paul's explanation is simply that God is God, and He doesn't have to explain Himself.

If that was all the Bible had to say about God's election, one might be satisfied, and that might be the end of the matter. It's as if a child were to go to his father and say "Dad, you set me up to fail, and I failed. So why do you blame me? Good question, right? But when dad answers "I'm your father and I don't have to explain myself," that ends the matter. You can argue further, but at that point you know it's over!. But the complication arises when Paul goes on in Chapter 10 to declare that the offer of salvation is held out to everyone, which is clearly contrary to what he has said in Chapter 9.

In Rom. 10, Paul uses the phrases "everyone who believes"; "If you confess, if you believe, you will be saved"; "Everyone who believes in him will not be put to shame"; "The Lord of all, bestows His riches on all who call on him"; "Everyone who calls on the name of the Lord will be saved."

In other words, I am unable to reconcile what are clearly two conflicting teachings of Paul. Why is this a problem? After all, it's not as if other areas of difficult scriptural truth are hard to grasp. I certainly recognize and accept mystery in Scripture—the trinity, for example. I can never hope to make logical sense out of one God in three persons. But that is a mystery, not a contradiction. But here, with election, we don't so much have a mystery as an outright contradiction. As distasteful as it seems, it is no mystery to me that God can create the human race for His glory and then pass over some of His created beings in salvation. As I say above, that is His prerogative as the Creator. But it is a contradiction to understand God as saying two opposite things—that He is the savior of the world but the savior of only the elect.

So, after all that, regarding the ordination process—on Sovereign Grace Church's statement of faith "Man's response to the gospel," it says:

> "Man's response to the gospel is rooted and grounded in the free and unconditional election of God for His own pleasure and glory. It is also true that the message of the gospel is only effectual to those who genuinely repent of their sins . . ."

I can't in all honesty support that statement, because it doesn't take into account the opposing truth, which is undeniable in Scripture (as reflected in the above verses in Rom. 10 and elsewhere)—that salvation is offered to everyone.

Secondly, the SGC Seven Shared Values, point #1 states

> ". . . we believe that God sovereignly chooses men and women to be saved . . . (Eph. 1:3–6, Rom. 9:11). God's sovereign grace in salvation . . . fills us with gratitude . . ."

Again, this statement is made to the exclusion of Scripture's truth that God extends salvation to all people. Also, to be honest, it does not fill me with gratitude to think about God's sovereign choice in election to the exclusion of those He has passed over. Can this thought truly be gratifying to anyone?

So where does this leave me? At this point, considering a lifetime of struggling with this issue, I would have to honestly say I understand election as only one side of a two-sided biblical teaching, both sides being equally true, yet contradicting each other.

For me, this stalemate is unsatisfying and deeply troubling. Yet it is where I find myself, in all honesty.

As it happened, although I never sent it, the letter helped me to solidify my thoughts enough to make the decision to end the process of ordination. The process of working through that dilemma led me to consider the wider phenomenon of thinking through the differences between trust and belief in the context of biblical faith.

Is Faith Trust Or Belief?

Another area of consideration is the relationship between *trusting* and *believing* in the context of one's faith. There's a beautifully poignant line in a short passage in J. R. R. Tolkien's *The Lord of the Rings*, just after Frodo and Strider meet, and Strider is trying to convince Frodo that the only way he would make it safely to his destination is to trust him and allow him to accompany Frodo on his journey, even though it seemed to Frodo that there was no good reason to trust him, not knowing anything about him. Strider tells Frodo that he would explain his story if it would help Frodo make up his mind. Then he adds: *"But why should you believe my story if you don't trust me already?"*

I've thought much about that same question in recent years in relation to God. I've lived most of my life under the assumption that believing in God has to precede trusting Him. And indeed, contrary to Tolkien's sensible point, that surely seems to be the biblical perspective—that belief precedes trust. So I've been conditioned all my life to think that when my belief would waver, it could only follow that my trust in God would decrease in proportion.

But think about it . . . there is an important and not so subtle difference between belief and trust. Belief is passive, it's something that *happens* to us. I either believe something *because it is believable*, or I don't believe it because it's not. That is, a proposition's quality of believability is a precondition of my believing it. Granted, there is an element of subjectivity in every act of belief. But as psychiatrist Victor Frankl put it, "You cannot will to believe." Expanding on that claim, Frankl writes: "If you want people to have faith and believe in God, you cannot rely on preaching along the lines of a particular church, but must, in the first place, portray your God believably."[82] What is unbelievable to me might be entirely believable to you. As author Gianni Vattimo explained it, "to believe means having faith, conviction, or certainty in something, but also to opine—that is, to think with a certain degree of uncertainty."[83] Richard Holloway regards faith as a "high risk," calling one to "embark on a hazardous course of action." He talks about "the mysterious way in which faith is chosen . . . A challenge to believe is, on the face of it, an odd thing to make. We either believe or we don't."[84]

Believing can actually mean two very different things: to have an opinion (right or wrong) about something; or to have conviction and certainty about something. We can hold our beliefs firmly and without wavering, or we can hold them lightly and without being obsessively fixated on them. In other words, we can believe something to be true without it making much difference to us, but we only place our faith in something that is crucial for the way we live. But in either case, believability is based on an outside influence rather than willful decision. There is no act of the will, no decision to be made. Do you believe the sun came up this morning? We don't say: "Let me think about it, and then I'll tell you whether I believe it or not."

But trust is a decision, an act of my will, usually, but not necessarily, based on whether belief is present, and not even always based on whether the

82. Victor Frankl, *The Unconscious God* (New York: Simon & Schuster, 1975), page 14.

83. Gianni Vattimo, *After Christianity* (New York: Columbia University Press, 2002), page 1.

84. Richard Holloway, *Crossfire: Faith and Doubt in an Age of Uncertainty* (Grand Rapids, MI: Eerdmans Publishing, 1988), page 27.

trust is merited. "Do you trust that chair to hold your weight?" It might or might not—I'll only know for sure if I test it. Based on my decision whether to trust or not, I'll either sit on the chair, or I won't. Just as Frodo had to decide whether to trust Strider *before* he believed his story, perhaps I should have good reason to trust God before fully believing particulars *about* him. As C. S. Lewis put it in his essay, "On Obstinacy in Belief":

> When you are asked for trust you may give it or withhold it; it is senseless to say that you will trust if you are given demonstrative certainty. There would be no room for trust if demonstration were given. When demonstration is given what will be left will be simply the sort of relation which results from having trusted, or not having trusted, before it was given.[85]

In other words, faith has so much more to do with trust than with belief. To say "I'm going to trust you," to someone who has not yet proved (to me) to be trustworthy is to throw myself at his mercy based on an incomplete weight of evidence. We do that every day in the ordinary affairs of life—I walk across the street trusting the driver of a car not to plow through a red light. I get in an elevator trusting that the cable won't snap; I committed to spend the rest of my life married to someone whom I trusted to be who I thought she was after dating for a few months.

And so with faith in God, we commit to placing our trust in a being we've never seen, whose voice we've never heard, but (we reason) one who has *progressively* proven Himself to be real and trustworthy, even as our *belief* in and about Him is imperfect. Dare I draw the obvious conclusion—the conclusion that I would venture to say we have all wondered about, some of us more often than others, but nevertheless all of us—that faith in God is a risk? If that question has never crossed your mind, even for a minute, I think it would be fair to question whether you have ever faced even a moment of grief or hardship to any degree.

---

85. C. S. Lewis, "On Obstinacy and Belief," page 28.

Another way to look at it is that having faith means to be convinced without seeing. Frederick Buechner puts it poetically:

> There will always be some who say that such faith is only a dream, and God knows there is none who can say it more devastatingly than we sometimes say it to ourselves . . . Faith is like a dream in which the clouds open to show such reaches ready to drop upon us that when we wake into the reality of nothing more than common sense, we cry to dream again because the dreaming seems truer than the waking does to the fullness of reality not as we have seen it, to be sure, *but as by faith we trust it to be without seeing.*[86] (italics added)

So what conclusion can be drawn from this dilemma between faith and belief? As I am writing from a place of indecision on my own journey, I realize that I am more sympathetic to honest doubt than I am to uncritical or unthinking belief in, or devotion to, the traditional truth claims that have been a part of my life for so many years. This conflict of faith that I've been describing has also been shaped by another important influence in my life: scholarship.

Faith And Scholarship

Much of my Christian worldview as an adult has been shaped by my having spent the last 30 years of my life as an Evangelical Christian employed in a secular (nonreligious) Jewish academic institution. I have formed some strong (and not surprisingly, critical) opinions about scholarship in general and about biblical/Judaic scholarship in particular. I'm sure what I'm about to say will sound excessively judgmental and perhaps even too much of a generalization. But to be honest, I'm not overstating what I think when I say that one of my biggest criticisms of the kind of high-level scholarship that goes on at an academic institution, like the one in which I've spent my career, is that the work that is produced is so far out of touch for the aver-

---

86. Frederick Buechner, *The Sacred Journey: A Memoir of Early Days* (New York: HarperCollins, 1982), page 57.

age person that it is virtually incomprehensible and useless to all but the specialists in the field. Granted, their purpose is to work at the highest level as scholars whose aim is to break new ground in their fields of research. And while I'm sure this happens to their satisfaction (and here comes the excessively judgmental part), I find that an extremely high percentage of the results of such scholarship—results that are disseminated by way of both lecture and print—is so abstruse, incomprehensible, and impractical that I wonder how these scholars can sustain interest in their own work. There! I've gotten that off my chest.

But more importantly, another criticism of modern scholarship is its inflated view of its own understanding of sacred recorded history. This is also a self-criticism about how my own thinking evolved in my student days. As previously mentioned, when I began my studies at Dropsie, it didn't take me long to come to the conclusion that the Bible is full of inaccuracies, and that only through the attempt to "restore" the text by means of critical scholarship could we come closer to a more accurate and fuller understanding of the Bible. Critical study assumes that the Bible is not a book that came about as a result of supernatural intervention, but rather it is just another book of history (albeit sacred history) containing errors, subject to "correction" by a more enlightened and technologically advanced readership, particularly by specialists in the field. How easy it was for me to evolve into the frame of mind of feeling more enlightened than the biblical writers. Come to think of it, how odd it was that I could so easily convince myself that sacred Scripture could remain sacred and still be inaccurate and full of error. Indeed, I remember a vivid encounter during that period of my life when—in a conversation with a minister about my newly "enlightened" views on the biblical text—he looked me in the eyes and said "stop editing the Bible and start reading it!"

Now, years after my graduate school days, I have come full circle, and although I am comfortable in recognizing that there are clearly elements of legend and myth in the Bible, I am also (somewhat, though not entirely) comfortable in seeing the whole Bible as God's message to humankind. And while I no longer accept the idea of plenary inspiration of Scripture (meaning that every word of Scripture is "God-breathed"), the various literary elements that went into composing the Bible do not conflict with my view of Scripture as sacred. At least I purpose to maintain and cultivate that way of regarding the text. That's not to deny that I live with a constant impulse to disregard as irrelevant or fanciful certain portions of Scripture that seem out of touch or nonsensical. On the contrary, it is a relentless battle to decide what should and shouldn't be considered as "sacred truth," regardless of my judgment about its historicity.

But here's an example that has stuck with me to illustrate my point about the general attitude of scholars about their own intellectual competency. Some years ago, the topic of one of our research years was a study of ancient Israelite religion. The goal of that year's study (as it is described in a 20-year published history of the Herbert D. Katz Center for Advanced Judaic Studies) was to "*escape* the romanticism and apologetics that have influenced the academic study of the Bible and ancient Israelite religion since its inception, and to *re-describe* the religion and culture of ancient Israel *in more accurate* and *less confessional terms*" (italics added).

Admittedly, I am conflicted here since modern scholarship, with the means at its disposal, as well as the advancement of methods of research that were not available to earlier scholarship, has clearly advanced knowledge. But, to be frank, there is a part of me that thinks it arrogant for modern scholars to consider the ancient account of a group of people, about their own world in which they lived, to be less accurate than an account of that group's history as reconstructed by scholars centuries after it was lived and written. As Ben Witherington put it, we need to "treat the Bible's authors with the respect they deserve and let them have their say in their own words, rather than trying to put words in their mouths. It is the height of arrogance to assume that only we in the 21st century are really in a position to understand these texts, and that 2,000 years of interpreters before us were all in the dark."[87] Again, while we should certainly recognize that modern scholarship, with the aid of computer technology, has developed tools that allow scholars to analyze ancient texts in ways that were impossible in the past,

---

87. Ben Witherington, *The Problem with Evangelical Theology* (Waco, TX: Baylor University Press, 2016).

nevertheless, my criticism is directed at the kind of skeptical scholarship that seeks to deconstruct any perspective in ancient writing that doesn't conform to modern scholars' "enlightened" viewpoint.

You will recall my mentioning earlier that I will present conflicting views of my own fluidity in thinking through these issues. Here is another example of where I see the conservative (Evangelical) viewpoint as having merit that I find it difficult to argue against: Modern biblical scholarship, prejudiced by denial of the supernatural, has virtually rewritten biblical history by positing the impossibility of the Bible's own claims to historical reliability and authorship. But consider this—it is abundantly clear that Jesus viewed the ancient biblical account as historically factual. He referenced Old Testament texts on several occasions to support His teaching. It's interesting, in fact, that Jesus references what is perhaps the most implausible narrative in the Old Testament—the story of Jonah—in a way that shows his belief in the historicity of the story. As Kevin DeYoung points out, isn't it more plausible to think Jesus knew Jewish history better then German critics almost 2,000 years later?[88] Honest biblical criticism (with the intent to restore the text rather than to destroy it) is a productive and worthy discipline. But I would claim that the approach of "deconstructionism" (the method of study that starts out with the assumption that the text is inaccurate and corrupt) is the single most destructive aspect of biblical scholarship.

But my greatest criticism of the kind of high-level scholarship I'm talking about is its ineffectiveness in impacting practical, everyday life, let alone religious life. Scholarship, as I have come to observe in my time working in an academic institution, is characterized by the pursuit of knowledge for its own sake. Not that there's anything objectionable about that, but my Evangelical coreligionists might argue as follows: The first three chapters of I Corinthians expand the idea of knowledge for its own sake so clearly. Paul uses expressions like "the foolishness of the message of the cross"; God choosing the "weak things to shame the strong"; "God's wisdom, secret

88. Kevin DeYoung, *Taking God at His Word: Why the Bible Is Knowable, Necessary, and Enough, and What That Means for You and Me* (Wheaton, IL: Crossway, 2014), page 106.

and hidden"; the "foolishness of preaching to save those who believe"; the "mystery of God as foolishness to those who are unspiritual"; and so on.

Paul's clear message here is that pursuit of knowledge that doesn't lead to a change of heart, leading to spiritual improvement, is un-useful at best, and wasteful and damaging at worst. I pursued, for a time in my life, this kind of knowledge. It consumed me during my two years of graduate study, and while I consider that time worthwhile in one way, I don't regret that it was cut short, for a variety of reasons. Paul writes later on in that same letter (chapter 13) ". . . though I understand all mysteries and all knowledge . . . and have not love, I am *nothing*." What a powerful indictment. I can't think of a more effective way to illustrate the futility of empty knowledge.

I stated earlier on that because my story is in progress, there are inevitable twists and turns in my faith journey even as I write. In dealing with the internal conflicts that naturally accompany any ongoing faith journey, I'm always looking for materials to read that explain and justify my doubts and also that refute and correct my thinking along the way. I recently came across a book in a thrift store that moved me to think about my diminishing view of things pertaining to my faith. I'm usually drawn directly to the used book section when I go to a thrift shop. Inevitably the shelves are filled with the modern popular fiction that people have read (or not) and discarded, but every once in a while, I'll find a book that captures my attention simply because it stands out from the usual useless reading material. Such was the case recently when I found a book written by a Christian activist and entitled *Finding God Beyond Harvard*.[89] In the book, Kelly Monroe Kullberg relates a story about her encounter in addressing a group of graduate students at a university where she was to speak on "The Bible and Feminism." Kelly relates how, through competent, patient, and respectful reasoning, an audience that had started out as arrogant and hostile gradually responded to her in kind, and what started as a chaotic, oppressive, and disruptive free-for-all turned out to be productive and thought-provoking for the audience. I was especially moved by the gradual change in the at-

---

89. Kelly Monroe Kullberg, *Finding God Beyond Harvard: The Quest for Veritas* (Downers Grove, IL: IVP Books, 2006), pages 66–81.

mosphere from one of hateful and abusive catcalls to one of thoughtful and positive interaction.

As I think about why that account moved me, it occurs to me that I am so often inclined to be part of that hostile and inflexible element that rejects the honest pursuit of faith. As I ask myself why that is, perhaps it's because it seems easier, less confrontational, and more intellectually stimulating to lean toward a position that moves me away from consideration of the supernatural element of faith. It reminds me of how, as I've already stated, I live and function in two worlds. In my "church" world, I'm surrounded by people of simple faith who express their views about life and spirituality in simple terms, black and white, moral or immoral, what I might call a simple dualism, where all thinking is measured against a biblical literalist worldview, and anything seemingly outside of that worldview is rejected as unworthy of thoughtful reflection. In that world, questions about morality and their answers are biblical, but simplistic. There's no room for debate because noncompliance to an established understanding of the text would represent doubt and unbelief—enemies of faith. For me, there must be a middle ground between the two extremes of the simplistic, literalist mindset of questioning nothing and the dishonest posture of questioning everything. I hope that this book is making the point that an honest questioning of everything is the most productive, if unsettling, place for a serious Christian seeker to be.

Faith And Exclusivity

I now finally come to my central argument—a topic that has been, for me, the most challenging biblical idea that I have wrestled with for many years, an idea of biblical authority that has been particularly troubling for me especially in recent years, and in fact one of the most perplexing Christian assertions that I've had to think through. I realize that the comments I'm about to make will cause concern for many people in my Evangelical circle, but to be transparent about my journey I have to deal with it. I'm referring to the exclusive nature of my faith—Christianity—that I am faced with in the New Testament.

Let me start by making a radical claim. To my knowledge, no other faith tradition besides Christianity teaches that there is no universal way to be acceptable to God except through the way prescribed by that faith (for us, salvation by grace alone, through faith alone in Jesus). Christianity is the only faith that makes that sort of claim. That fact in itself would not, of course, be a strong enough argument *not* to embrace it. For if that claim to exclusivity could somehow suddenly and unarguably be proved to be true so that it would be evident to everyone, then not to embrace it would be insanity. And, in fact, for Evangelical Christianity that is exactly the case—the exclusive nature of the New Testament's call to saving faith, as expounded most unambiguously by the Apostle Paul, is indisputable. Here's how Richard Holloway represents the Christian claim:

> The desire to belong to a gang, an exclusive community, particularly one that is blessed with knowledge that is hidden from others, is potentially attractive to many . . . Christian theological history is filled with stories of groups who have developed theories of the election of themselves to salvation and the damnation of others; theories that demonstrate that their particular group has been exclusively endowed with divine truth, so that they possess a unique mission to the world and have a unique authority within it. Claims of this sort have been held and are still held by Christians.[90]

Perhaps no one has made my point better than the Jewish philosopher Franz Rosenzweig, who not only appreciated Christianity, but regarded it as a valid faith alongside his own. Ronald Miller, in his book on Rosenzweig,[91] discusses the problem of supersessionism (the idea that Christianity doesn't complement Judaism but actually replaces or displaces it). The point that stands out to me is that, although no Christian with even the slightest historical knowledge would deny that the Christian faith arose out of Judaism and obviously owes its roots to Judaism, that is where Judaism's usefulness to Christianity ends for most Christians. In other words, the

---

90. Richard Holloway, *Doubts and Loves: What is Left of Christianity* (Edinburgh, UK: Canongate Books Ltd., 2001), page 156.

91. Ronald Miller, *Dialogue and Disagreement: Franz Rosenzweig's Relevance to Contemporary Jewish-Christian Understanding* (Lanham, MD: University Press of America, 1990).

church acknowledges its Judaic roots, but sees little if any significance to the Jewish faith over the past 2,000 years, at least with regard to the question, "How does man approach God?" In fact, to the contrary, in general, the church understands Judaism's significance only in a negative way, as an example of unbelief and as a means for the "new elect" to gain access to God's kingdom. In other words, Christianity's success is only made possible by Judaism's failure. Ronald Miller represents the prevailing Christian position accurately when he writes:

> Christianity has said a great deal about Judaism in its two thousand-year history. But in these instances Judaism has inevitably been defined in terms of Christianity's own identity and faith . . . Judaism was constantly Christianity's foil, the scapegoat for Christianity's failures in faith, the projection of Christianity's shadow . . . Christianity's good news, in other words, was always simultaneously a bad news for the Jews.[92]

Hans Küng calls this a "pseudo-theology which reinterpreted the Old Testament salvation history of the Jewish people, overlooking the permanent election of this people asserted by Paul and relating it exclusively to Christians as the 'New Israel.'"[93] As I'll discuss below, although Paul defended the idea of Israel's permanent election, he himself was conflicted and therefore failed to make a convincing case since he reinterpreted Old Testament texts to prove the exact opposite: that Israel's special election was in fact not permanent. (See the following section: "Paul's Misapplication of Old Testament Scripture").

John Gager, who characterizes the New Testament as blatantly anti-Semitic, sees the problem as "a profound theological crisis in which nothing less than faith itself is at stake."[94] Gager makes a concise but strong argument against Christianity's view that Judaism has been replaced or super-

---

92. Ronald Miller, *Dialogue and Disagreement: Franz Rosenzweig's Relevance to Contemporary Jewish-Christian Understanding* (Lanham, MD: University Press of America, 1990), page 122.

93. Hans Küng, *On Being a Christian* (New York: Doubleday, 1976), page 170.

94. John Gager, *The Origins of Anti-Semitism: Attitudes Toward Judaism in Pagan and Christian Antiquity* (London: Oxford University Press, 1983), page 33.

seded by Christianity. He states three conditions, all of which are true of
early Christianity:

1. If a religious community [Christianity] views its legitimacy as fundamentally dependent on an authority that is also claimed by another religious community [Judaism's Hebrew Scripture]

2. If this other religious community [Judaism] presents arguments that establish its claims (continuity of ritual observance, use of Scriptures in the original language . . .)

3. If this other religious community flourishes and exercises an appeal among the faithful of the new religion [as 1st-century Judaism clearly did]

Then, rather than motivating the new religion to supplant the old faith, these factors should inevitably lead the new religion to recognize its moral debt to the old religion. Sadly, the opposite happened. Rather than recognize its debt to Judaism, in an effort to establish and affirm itself as a new religion that was "better" than Judaism, Christianity grew to see Judaism as a failed religion, unable to claim the universality of the new faith. Rather than understanding Judaism as a continuing dynamic and living faith, it came to be judged, in the eyes of early Christianity, as an incomplete and unfulfilled faith, incapable of standing on its own. Alan Davies foresees an even more somber consequence of the problem:

> It may be that the Church will survive if we fail to deal adequately with that question, but more serious is the question whether the Church ought to survive. A Christian Church with an anti-Semitic New Testament is abominable, but a Christian Church without a New Testament is inconceivable.[95]

The problem is not whether or not Christianity's claim of exclusivity is supported in Scripture. It couldn't be clearer on the basis of the New Tes-

---

95. Alan Davies, *Antisemitism and the Foundations of Christianity* (Mahwah, NJ: Paulist Press, 1979), page 48.

tament evidence. Jesus's teaching about Himself leaves no ambiguity about the exclusive nature of his claim to be the only means of approach to God. Even these two Scriptures alone state the claim clearly and simply: *"I am the way, the truth, and the life, no man comes to the father but by me."* (John 14:6), and Peter is just as clear when he says *"There is no other name under heaven, given among men by which we must be saved"* (Acts 4:12).

Rather, the challenge lies in the reality that the Bible *as a whole* is not nearly as clear-cut in teaching a message of exclusive salvation through Jesus as the Messiah as Evangelical Christianity makes it out to be. I would articulate the point like this: The Bible was composed over a history spanning more than 1,700 years (assuming the earliest date for Mosaic authorship of the Torah). So we read the Bible today with the benefit of seeing how God worked through history from creation through the first century after Jesus walked the earth. In that long historical account (outlined briefly in what follows), we can see God acting upon history and interacting with His creation in different ways.

A brief historical summary

The message of the Old Testament (or more accurately, the Christian interpretation of the Old Testament message) can be summarized as follows: God created an innocent and sinless race of humanity through Adam and Eve to live in harmony with Himself. Adam and Eve very soon destroyed their sinless nature by disobeying God's clear guidelines through an act of free will, contaminating the entire human race with sin, bringing separation between God and humanity. Eventually the sinfulness of humankind became so widespread that God obliterated the entire human race by means of a worldwide deluge—with the exception of the family of Noah, whom He preserved.

A few generations after Noah's family brings us to Abraham, a man who, for no apparent reason "finds grace in God's eyes" and is selected to be the father of a family God claims as his "chosen nation." God now has a special group of people He selected out of all of humanity to be treated with special care, to be privileged to be God's one and only chosen people. God

sets His affection on the Jews and leaves no doubt that it is an exclusive relationship He has established with them. I mean he *really* leaves no doubt,
fighting one holy war after another on behalf of the Israelites against their
enemies, leaving us with the impression of a God who, once He has made
up His mind whom He favors, is merciless to any and all other nations that
challenge that choice.

The covenant by which God unites Himself to His chosen people is based
on a very special kind of bond—the bond of *hesed*, a reciprocal relationship
that cannot be broken. This *hesed* relationship between God and the Israelites is the foundation of their status as God's permanent chosen people (for
example, in Exodus 34:6–7, and more graphically in Hosea 2:16–23). (For
more on this, see my article on "Ruth and Hesed" in the Selected Writings,
page 162) But this chosen people eventually (rather quickly, as we see in the
beginning of Judges) turns its back on God and breaks their side of the
bargain (or the covenant). The expectation would be for God to release
Himself from the covenant—to "be off the hook" so to speak, in keeping
His side of the bargain, to let them go their own way and move on to place
his affections on another, "more deserving" group of people.

But that's not what God does. Rather, He holds on to his chosen people—after all, this is a *hesed* covenant, unbreakable. So as we see in the
prophets (particularly Jeremiah 31 and elsewhere), not only is God faithful
to keep His bond with people who have broken a seemingly unbreakable
relationship, but He also declares that "all Israel will be saved." Paul too
(Rom 10–11, especially vv. 26–32) makes it clear that "all Israel" (that is,
the Jewish nation) will be saved.

Now, the problem lies in the obvious conflict between God's unbreakable
bond with His chosen covenant people and the apparent breaking of that
bond that we see later in Scripture, where God seems to change His mind
and redirects His affections onto a completely new object—namely those
individuals who would call on His name from every nation. The obvious
question is: Why the drastic change? How and why does that resolute bond
between God and His exclusive, called-out nation (that unbreakable *hesed*
bond, which guaranteed permanent status of unconditional "chosen-ness")

now morph into a general call to individuals outside of the nation of Israel? How is one to understand God's apparent breaking of that bond with the Israelites? Are they no longer the treasured people of God? Did God change His mind? And if so, why?

This, to me, is the core dilemma or challenge that one faces as a biblical interpreter. There are a few typical Evangelical arguments used to navigate and mitigate this problem, none of which are completely satisfactory. One argument says that it's simply not true, that it is a misreading or misrepresentation of the Gospels and Paul's letters to claim that God broke His bond with Israel. The problem here is that Scripture as a whole gives conflicting answers to the question whether God has given up on Israel as His elect people. For example, in Jeremiah 3:8: *"For all the adulteries of that faithless one, Israel, I had sent her away with a decree of divorce . . ."* Or Jesus's parable in Matthew 21:43: *"The kingdom of God will be taken away from you and given to a people that produces the fruits of the kingdom."* Texts like this fly in the face of other Scriptures (like the ones quoted above) that declare God's unrelenting promise to His chosen nation.

Even Paul himself (who dealt in more depth than any other biblical writer with the question of Israel as God's elect) gives conflicting viewpoints. While Paul clearly states in Romans 11 that God *did not* give up on Israel (*"Has God rejected his people? By no means!"*), he seems to be saying the very opposite in the same letter (Rom. 9): *"Not all Israelites truly belong to Israel, and not all of Abraham's children are his true descendants . . ."* Can the conflict, even within Paul himself, be any more obvious? Paul here is making a claim upon which he will build his entire argument of replacement theology. The only problem is that the premise of his claim is false, pure and simple. Contrary to his audacious claim that "not all Israelites belong to Israel," the glaringly obvious fact is that, of course, *all* Israelites *do* belong to Israel. And even more obvious—of course *all* of Abraham's children are his true descendants. I'll explore this point further below.

Another popular Christian argument to counter the idea that God changed His mind says that those who were saved before Jesus were saved somehow by a sort of prophetic "looking forward" to Jesus's saving work. Probably the most popular Scripture used as a proof text for this idea is Genesis 15:6, which Paul uses as his proof text in Romans 4: "What then shall we say that Abraham our father has found according to the flesh? For if Abraham was justified by works, he has something to boast about, but not before God. For what does the Scripture say? *'Abraham believed God, and it was accounted to him for righteousness.'"*

I never understood how this argument made any sense as a text to prove salvation by grace in the Old Testament. The text states that Abraham was declared righteous because "he believed God" *for an heir*, not because he put his faith in what Jesus would accomplish 1,700 years later. Furthermore, God's declaration of Abraham as righteous does not demand the meaning that proponents of the interpretation would give it. Rather, Abraham was simply regarded by God as "righteous" in the sense that his belief in God's promise was a righteous act—a virtuous and upright response in God's eyes. Secondly, why apply this to future generations at all? The implication of such an argument would be that anyone and everyone in any generation since Abraham who believes God *for any promise at all* is considered to be exercising faith for salvation, just like Abraham. But of course that's not the message or implication of Abraham's faith, and it's not the message of the gospel of salvation. Rather, the gospel message is specifically exercising faith in the atoning work of Jesus that qualifies one for salvation.

A third Evangelical argument goes something like this: When God says "all Israel will be saved," he doesn't really mean "every" Jew, but rather is making a statement about those whom Paul names "true Jews," whom he defines as those who are not Jews outwardly (in the flesh) but from a promise (Romans 9). This is where the matter becomes even more conflicted because if we stop reading at the end of Romans 9, we have an incomplete picture of what is happening. What seems to be clearly implied through the end of Romans 9 is that Paul is drawing a conclusion about the Jews that is completely contrary to the Old Testament facts. Paul is clearly saying that "spiritual" Jews are more "Jewish" than natural Jews, and that the clear Old Testament teaching of God's choice to call out, from all of His creation, an actual physical, permanent, and specific ethnic group was not really what God had intended to do and that when God said "I will make an everlasting covenant with them" (Jeremiah 32:40), He didn't really mean "everlasting," and he didn't really mean "with them" (the people of Israel). It seems, in other words, that Paul stretches the meaning of the biblical texts to the point where his theology renders God's original purpose as null and void. So, no longer does God intend to hold on to physical Israel as he so clearly and unambiguously promises in the Torah and the Prophets. Rather, it is as if God changed His mind, broke His promise, gave up on saving the Israelites as a whole, and changed the definition of who constitutes "Israel."

To be truly Evangelical demands at this point that one take the position that says God chose a nation of people to be singled out among all the people of the earth to be His *permanent* and special possession, made an eternal covenant with that nation, a calling that turned out *not to be permanent* after all. A careful reading of the biblical texts that Paul uses cannot possibly lead to Paul's conclusion.

Clearly two opposing "truths" emerge when one looks at the complete picture. Only by the use of creative license can one put this puzzle together, and one is hard pressed to satisfactorily reconcile what are clearly two opposing truths about one of the most important conundrums of Scripture: election of Israel and rejection of Israel.

As I alluded to above, the typical method Evangelicals used to reconcile this problem is an argument that goes as follows: God's covenant with Israel was conditioned on Israel's faithfulness to Him. When Israel failed, God was not obligated to honor His side of the covenant promise. But not only does this teaching completely obliterate the terms of the *hesed* relationship, which, as I pointed out above, is permanent. But since the thought of God abandoning His chosen people is somehow an abhorrent idea for us, we go through the mental gymnastics of positing the theory that it has always been part of God's plan that Israel's rejection was God's intent all along, in order to reveal to all of humanity their need of salvation. Using Paul's creative reasoning, especially in Romans 9–11, we come to posit a "replacement theology" in which selection, rejection, and replacement was always God's plan. But when we look more closely at Romans 9–11, especially in

light of the Old Testament Scriptures that Paul references there, we find
quite a different picture.

Paul's Misapplication Of Old Testament Scripture

I realize that the heading of this section presents a bold challenge to Christianity's cherished idea of biblical infallibility. But it can't be avoided since
Paul, more than any other New Testament writer, dealt with the question
of God's making and breaking of his covenant with the Jews. Let's take a
close look at his argument as a whole. Realizing that I am challenging or
questioning Paul's very meticulous reasoning, I don't see how questions
that seem to be so obvious can be avoided. Let's see where the argument
leads as we let Paul speak for himself.

Romans 9 starts by defining Israel and detailing exactly what God's covenant with the Israelites means, highlighting the idea of closeness and possession (v. 3–5):

1. Israelites are "adopted as sons."

2. The covenant belongs to them.

3. The law, the temple, and the promises are theirs.

4. The messiah comes from their line.

But then Paul immediately, in v. 6, declares the opposite—distance and
disinheritance: "They are not all Israel who are descended from Israel." And
in what follows, he builds what seems to be a solid case for his new definition of "Israel" that expands beyond the ethnic nation, pointing out that
Abraham and Isaac had children who were not counted in the line of Israel
(namely Ishmael and Esau). But we are immediately confronted with the
obvious point (a point that Paul himself makes) that there *were* children
of Abraham and Isaac who carried on the physical line of Israel (v.7–13).
However, Paul pulls a bait and switch as he references the non-Jewish ge-
nealogies of Abraham and Isaac (through Ishmael and Esau) to open the

door that will lead to his conclusion that Israel's permanent election was not God's intent.

Let's take a close look at the Scriptures that Paul uses to make this point. Paul cites three Old Testament texts to support his argument that the theology of the Hebrew authors naturally finds fulfillment in Paul's theological understanding in Romans 9. The only problem is that a simple but careful reading of each of these Old Testament texts reveals the very opposite of what Paul is trying to prove. As will become clear, Paul's interpretations of the Old Testament texts that he cites in Romans 9 reveal inconsistencies in his reasoning, due to his misinterpretation of the Old Testament texts or (more likely) his selective reading into the texts ideas that were clearly not the intent of the writers of those texts.

Text #1—Rom. 9:15–22 (Referencing Exodus 33:19):

Paul's attempt to show that Israel was not God's permanent possession.

First, in v. 15, Paul references Exodus 33:19: *"I will have mercy on whom I will have mercy . . . ,"* and he comes to a surprising conclusion (Rom 9:22) that, based on that text, God's original plan was to replace Israel as the object of His affection: *"What if God, although willing to demonstrate His wrath and to make His power known, endured with much patience vessels of wrath prepared for destruction . . . that He might make known the riches of His glory upon vessels of mercy, which He also prepared beforehand for glory . . ."* But his proof text, Exodus 33, rather than declaring God's intent to replace Israel with those "on whom He would have mercy," is clearly showing God's intent to do just the opposite: to call out the nation of Israel as a *permanent* possession, to have mercy on Israel among all of the nations:

- God singled out Moses by name (v. 12).

- The nation of Israel is God's people (v. 13).

- God's people have gained God's favor (v. 15).

PART THREE: Journey Toward Faith

Then Exodus 34 and following are all about the details of God's special relationship with Israel. In other words, Paul's very use of Exodus 33—to prove that God had always intended to change the object of His saving grace—proves the exact opposite.

Text #2—Rom. 9:24-26 (Referencing Hosea 2:25):

This is Paul's attempt to change the definition of who constitutes "God's people."

Paul references Hosea to make his point that the covenant is obsolete. He cites Hosea 2:25, "I will call those who were not my people 'my people,'" and he applies this statement of Hosea to Gentiles (Rom 9:24). But let's look more closely at the Hosea passage—he lays out his overall prophetic message about Israel's fate in chapters 1–3, through a picture of marriage, adultery, and divorce—an argument that runs as follows: Because Israel, God's bride, has committed spiritual adultery, she is divorced (2:4, "I am not her husband"). Then, in that compelling picture of the abandoned husband wooing his wayward bride back to himself in Hosea 2:16–25, picturing the eventual full and permanent restoration of the Israelites as God's people, the prophet concludes with that statement quoted by Paul: "I will call those who were not my people, My people." Hosea clearly has in mind the return of ethnic *national* Israel as God's people (not a new people) *returning* to her husband. Hosea's sense here is completely unambiguous. But Paul applies the verse to a *new* (non-Israelite) people whom God would take for Himself, making His point in the strongest language (Rom 9:30–33), where he concludes that the Gentiles succeeded in gaining God's favor where Israel failed.

Paul's blatant misapplication of the obvious point being made in Hosea is too clear to miss. I am not claiming that Paul's application of the story of Hosea's restored wife to apply to the church was not true to Paul's intended purpose in Romans. Clearly it was! What one cannot avoid seeing, however, is that Paul's application of the Hosea story to the church is not the *exclusive* meaning, or even the primary meaning, of the Hosea story. In other words, God's purpose to restore national, physical Israel should not be denied simply because Paul applies it to the Gentiles coming into God's favor. Paul is concerned in Romans 9 with only one aspect of Hosea's story: how it applies to God's plan to bring to Gentiles a share in Israel's blessings. Replacement theology would teach (quite to the contrary) that national Israel ceases at this point to have any place in God's plan.

Text #3—Rom. 9:27–29 (Referencing Isaiah 1:9):

Paul's identification of the Israelite remnant with Gentile believers

Finally, Paul cites his third prophetic text to show God's replacement of national Israel with individual Gentiles (Isaiah 1:9): "Unless the Lord of Hosts had left us some survivors, we should be like Sodom . . ." And who are the survivors here in question? According to Paul, it is Gentile believers. But following Isaiah's prophetic discourse in chapters 1–12 it most certainly is not Gentile believers—rather it is clearly the remnant of physical and national Israel that is the remnant in Isaiah's mind. And Isaiah's prophecy, taken as a whole, confirms this, culminating in that most famous of texts, Isaiah 40: ". . . comfort, comfort *my people*, says your God . . . her warfare has ended, her iniquity has been removed . . ."

In summary, Paul is taking the liberty of applying to Gentile believers Old Testament Scriptures that are particularly and *exclusively* about Israel. Evangelical Christians accept Paul's use of Scriptures as Scripture for us. Our view of inspiration and preservation of Scripture not only allows us to view that as a legitimate means of bringing new truth, it *demands* it. We don't set out with a preconceived purpose to question Paul's creative application of these Old Testament texts. Rather, the Christian view of the unity of all of Scripture demands that we accept that Paul's interpretive understanding of the Old Testament texts is integral in the overall flow of the New Testament message.

But the problem is even more serious: When we follow Paul's argument in Romans 10 it seems that he is taking a step beyond the *inclusion* of Gentiles in promises made to Israel, and he actually declares Israel's special election obsolete (v. 12): "For there is no distinction between Jew and Greek." Really? How can Paul justify such a statement in direct contradiction to the immense volume of the Old Testament that is devoted specifically to just that: Israel as God's distinct people? In short, the three texts cited above are clearly expressing the very opposite of what Paul interprets them to be saying.

But in spite of what clearly seem to be misapplications of Old Testament texts, if we follow Paul's whole argument to its conclusion, surprisingly, he turns around on his own prior claims by clearly defending the salvation of the ancestral nation of Israel rather than "spiritual Israel," for he goes on to say, in chapter 11, that actual physical Israel (the "root") will be saved (11:26). And in that wonderfully graphic conclusion that closes his argument (11:27–33), Paul reinforces this truth when he says (11:29) that ". . . the gifts and callings of God are irrevocable." If God's calling out of Israel as His special chosen possession is irrevocable (which, again, Paul is clearly saying it is) then Paul's own prior argument of a replacement of that calling with a new and different kind of calling (to individual salvation) is an outright contradiction of his own argument.

Verses 33–34 of Romans 11 leave us with the only honest conclusion that can be drawn, in fact, a conclusion that relieves us of the tension created by Paul's seemingly contradictory argument: "Oh the depth of the riches both of the wisdom and knowledge of God! How unsearchable are His judgments and His ways past finding out! For who has known the mind of the Lord?" In other words, even after his own drawn-out explanation of how non-Jews are folded into God's covenantal promises to the Jews, Paul himself comes to a point in his theology where he simply concedes that he doesn't know how all this will play out. And so it should be when we muse over the mysteries of God. Paul himself was mystified by his own reasoning, as he himself admitted in the text just cited (Romans 11:33–34). With that in mind, it becomes unrealistic to hold to a theology that says there is no special future redemptive hope for the nation of Israel apart from the incorporation of individual Jews into the newly established kingdom of Jesus.

Having spent much of my adult life studying Scripture, living in both worlds (my Evangelical Christian world and my Jewish academic world) and observing the religiosity in both worlds, I can only reject a theology that nullifies a prior established covenantal relationship (i.e., God's "calling out of the Jews as a special possession"), as well as a theology that incorporates a new group (individual Gentiles) into the promises made exclusively to a national entity (biblical Israel). As I said earlier, it seems more reasonable to posit a God who is more creative and versatile, not restricted to a narrow method of conducting His relations with His created world, a God whose reach extends across the world that He created in ways that don't restrict the possibility of that entire created world participating in the benefits of His grace. In short, it seems most like a God of love to also be a God of inclusion, rather than exclusion, a God who is creative enough to present multiple ways of grace to the multiplicity of humanity. As I've tried to show, much of the biblical evidence (especially Paul's writing) portrays a God whose selective and shifting dealings with humanity seem ambiguous and conflicted. That portrayal falls far short of the image of a universally beneficent and great God who cares for the entirety of His created world. In the end, I can only conclude that one must come to the point where (like Paul, who, in spite of his contradictory reasoning) we stop and consider, "Who can know the mind of God?"

Faith Journey Through Later Life

Having discussed some of the rather weighty theological issues that have occupied my thinking, I now return to my own story to talk about some practical ways those issues have worked out in more recent years.

My father passed away on April 30, 2014, at the old age of 89. I've thought a lot about him and about the idea of "afterlife" over the past few years since he died. Rather than dwell on thoughts about his death as a sad event to be filed away in my memory, my thoughts often turned to questions having to do with the here and now of his existence, questions I wish could be asked and answered, such as: "What is it like to be going through the process of dying, knowing that you will soon exit this life and (assuming there's an afterlife) enter into a completely different sphere of existence?"

"What was going through my father's mind in those last moments when we held his hand and said our goodbyes for the last time, releasing him into the eternal unknown?" "What has become of him, if anything, since his passing?"

"What (again, if anything) is dad doing right now?" "What's he thinking about?"

"Who is he spending time with?" "Is he enjoying reunion with his siblings?" "Is he getting to know my other friends who have passed on"?

"Is he looking down at me?" "Is he lonely for his wife of 60-plus years?" And more . . .

For a time after his passing, as I mused over these kinds of questions, I lived with a strong sense of his ongoing presence, along with a persistent desire to communicate with him. He continues to be very much alive to me in my thoughts about him. His passing has given me occasion to think more deeply about the fragility of life and how that might (or should) compel me to live more purposefully.

Thinking about my father's death also causes me to think more about my own mortality. The one thing about my future that I'm sure about (really the only thing) is that I will most certainly die and pass, like my father, into that "eternal unknown." But the more I think about it, the more contented I find myself in accepting its inevitability. And indeed, the closer I get to it, I find that I am less and less anxious about it or troubled by the thought of it.

The best book I've read on the subject of death is *Love is Stronger than Death*[96] by Peter Kreeft, in which he describes five stages of experience on the journey toward—and in the process of thinking through—our relationship with death, starting with death as an enemy and culminating in death as a lover. With every fiber of our being, we strive every minute of every

---

96. Peter Kreeft, *Love is Stronger than Death* (San Francisco: Ignatius Press, 1979).

day, instinctually, to live, and at the same time we are constantly avoiding the thought of our progression toward inevitable death. But I'm not talking about merely longing for existence versus nonexistence. Animals have that instinct, as well as we humans do. Rather, I believe our true yearning for life and for seeing death as an enemy is our instinct for immortality.

I believe that a gradual change of heart occurs as part of the aging process. I've seen it happen with my own mother, and I sense a hint of the same phenomenon beginning to stir in my own soul. I'm not talking about callous acceptance of the inevitability of death—that is an absurdity. The will to live is active in all of us, no matter what condition or stage of life we are in. Even in the midst of the most inhumane and hopeless state, as Holocaust survivor Victor Frankl famously wrote: "Those who have a 'why' to live, can bear with almost any 'how.'"[97] But I do believe that there is a subtle and gradual but sure change of heart that stirs inside over the idea of the fear of death.

A few factors come to mind when I pursue or explore the thought process. For me, perhaps it has to do with a sense of having completed the most crucial years in providing for the recipients of my care. Even though I most certainly desire to be able to experience many more years of loving and supporting my children and grandchildren, it is no longer an essential responsibility—they'll be just fine without me. Or perhaps I'm starting to come to terms with the certainty that I will never fully come to the point of satisfaction of a completely fulfilled and well-lived life, which is not to say I should stop working and striving toward that end. But it seems important to gradually become comfortable knowing that I will never succeed in accomplishing all my desires and life goals. Far from it—and it seems to me that perhaps the sooner I recognize that reality, the more prepared I think I will be to deal with the end of life.

Another thought that has been stirring inside is the desire to be able to say something important upon my departure from my loved ones. As my father was nearing death, there was one occasion, about three or four months

97. Victor Frankl, *Man's Search for Meaning* (New York: Penguin Books, 1968)

before the end, when our family was gathered together for Thanksgiving. We all sat transfixed as he spoke directly to us—grandchildren included—words of wisdom, the likes of which we had not heard come from his lips up until that point. It was a profound experience for all of us. What I remember most about it was that it was genuinely uncharacteristic of him to talk to us that way. Although he wasn't able to think clearly—the cancer in his body had by that time gone to his brain—he spoke more boldly, more eloquently, though somewhat disjointedly due to the cancer, than I had ever heard him speak. He voiced thoughts that were beyond the realm of his usual expression, as if he were midway between earth and heaven in what he was thinking and feeling and seeing.

It was truly an amazing spiritual moment in the life of our family that none of us who were in the room will forget. It seemed very much like that scene in *The Brothers Karamazov* when Alyosha talks about how Father Zosima spoke in his dying hour:

> . . . although he spoke distinctly and in a sufficiently firm voice, his talk was rather incoherent. He spoke of many things, he seemed to want to say everything, to speak one last time before the moment of death, to say all that had not been said in his life, and not only for the sake of instruction, but as if he wished to share his joy and ecstasy with all, to pour out his heart once more in this life.[98]

Later on, in his last few days, our dad was unable to speak more than a word here and there, but I knew that he was thinking thoughts—lofty and otherworldly thoughts—that I wished I could hear him express, thoughts that I knew would be so good and beneficial for us to hear and remember. My heart's desire is to be, for my loved ones, as my father was for us when he neared death. I want to have the opportunity to speak with a fresh level of authority and certitude about the spiritual thoughts that I hope I will be privileged to be thinking as I transition out of this life to whatever comes next. I hope that I will be in a state of mind that will allow me to reject

98. Fyodor Dostoevsky, *The Brothers Karamazov* (New York: Farrar, Straus and Giroux, 1990), p. 163.

the inclination, the urge, to go inward and think about myself in those last moments, but rather to speak directly to those around me about what I believe will be a heightened sensitivity toward the supernatural realities that (I hope) I will be privileged to know at that moment. And with that comes a present reminder of how I wish to avoid living inward and self-centered in the here and now, but to live outward even to the end.

Still, having said that, my most fascinating thought about death is the whole idea of uncertainty about what lies beyond. I truly believe that most people, even most of my fellow believing Christians—if they were hard-pressed to give an honest response—would have to admit what is no less than a verifiable fact, undeniably 100 percent true, which is this: Regardless of all the books written about the experiences of people claiming to have gone to heaven and back, regardless of what you believe, regardless even of what the Bible says, we are simply not privileged to know the mystery of what happens after death. While the transition between life and death is the most fundamentally real transition in human experience, there is an unbridgeable gap in our understanding of the passage across that threshold. That is not a negative way of thinking about what lies beyond. On the contrary, it is a stirring and exciting reality. I can, in fact, stir one toward faith and hope.

The Strongest Argument For Faith And Hope

Perhaps that's why the Bible talks about heaven as a "hope." That also explains why philosophers have devised "proofs" for God's existence or for heaven. If it were self-evident, it wouldn't require proof. And that brings me to my own favorite "explanation" for God and heaven: the idea of hope, which, although it is not a proof (since I think I've proved, at least to myself, that we can't prove God), it is the most satisfactory *evidence*, and in fact a very satisfying one. Where does hope really come from?

C. S. Lewis writes about hope in several of his works—he expresses the idea of *Sehnsucht*, the German word that, while difficult to translate, basically describes a deep emotional state of "longing," "yearning," or "craving," or in a wider sense a type of "intensely missing." While the idea of *Sehnsucht* appears throughout C. S. Lewis's works, my two favorite expressions of the idea in his work are in his allegory *The Pilgrim's Regress*, and in his essay "The Weight of Glory."

As C. S. Lewis's character Wisdom (in *The Pilgrim's Regress*) says: "Let us conclude then that what you desire is no state of yourself at all, but something, for that very reason, Other and Outer. And knowing this, you will find tolerable the truth that you cannot attain it . . . Anything that you could have would be so much less than this that its fruition would be below the mere hunger, for this Wanting is better than having."[99] Or again: "You already know that the objects which your desire imagines are always inadequate to that desire. Until you have it you will not know what you wanted."[100] This desire or yearning is so elusive, as Lewis puts it, that most people discover it in themselves as a desire that cannot be satisfied. It's worth lingering on this idea in Lewis for a moment because it is so important. In what follows, I give a rather lengthy account of Lewis's and Kreeft's thinking on this subject because it is so meaningful to me as part of my personal faith journey. To paraphrase Peter Kreeft, you either see it or you don't. If it doesn't speak to you, skip over it.

In C. S. Lewis's classic essay "The Weight of Glory" (an absolute must-read for anyone who seeks to understand the heart of Lewis) he describes in vivid language the sense of yearning that is so strong in us that it can hardly be put into words. To quote just a few lines:

"The power of desiring is itself a reward."

[There is] in each one of us . . . a secret we cannot hide and cannot tell, thought we desire to do both. We cannot tell it because it is a desire for something that has never actually appeared in our

---

99. Lewis, C. S. *The Pilgrim's Regress* (Grand Rapids, MI: Eerdmans Publishing, 1943), pages 129–130.

100. Ibid, page 160.

experience. We cannot hide it because our experience is constantly
suggesting it.

"We remain conscious of a desire that no happiness will satisfy."

Richard Holloway expressed it this way: "The existence of a longing or
appetite does not prove the existence of its satisfaction, but it would be a
strange universe that produced longings as wildly unrealistic as the longings of religion unless something out there corresponded to them in some
way."[101]

Peter Kreeft develops Lewis's "Argument from Desire" for God's existence,
but he actually goes back to an argument of Thomas Aquinas:

> It is impossible for natural desire to be unfulfilled, since "nature
> does nothing in vain." Now, natural desire would be in vain if it
> could never be fulfilled. Therefore, man's natural desire is capable
> of fulfillment, but not in this life . . . So, it must be fulfilled after
> this life. Therefore, man's ultimate felicity comes after this life.

Here is Kreeft's excellent retelling of the "Argument from Desire." I give it
in some detail because it is so stirring, at least for me. The argument has
two premises and a conclusion:

1. Every natural, innate desire in us corresponds to some real object
   that can satisfy that desire.

2. But there exists in us a desire which nothing in time, nothing on
   earth, no creature can satisfy.

Therefore there must exist something more than time, earth and
creatures, which can satisfy this desire. This something is what people call "God" or "life with God forever."

Kreeft explains that there are two types of desires: externally conditioned desires and innate universal desires. Externally conditioned desires are those desires that come from outside us. They come from something accidental and culturally relative and are, therefore, artificial and vary from person to person. For example, a person may desire the Land of Oz or to fly like Superman. These desires, however, only exist based on an artificial imprint from a movie or a comic book. They therefore do not correspond to a reality, and certainly not to a common human desire. However, the innate universal desires all correspond to something real and are all desires that are common to the human experience. These desires consist of things such as food, drink, sex, knowledge, and beauty. To prove if a desire is innate, one only need ask if it is universal (in time, space, and to all humanity). The distinction between the two types of desires is helpful to distinguish desires as they correspond to their objects. From here, one is able to posit the second premise—that there exists in us a desire that nothing in time or space can satisfy, and that this desire (as a natural, innate desire) corresponds to a real object. There is a desire that stands out from all others, which is radically different, not in degree, but in kind—the desire of *Sehnsucht*, that deep, mysterious longing. There are two characteristics that distinguish this desire: 1) the desire has never been satisfied, and 2) the deep longing is painful, yet pleasurable at the same time. Of the first characteristic, when one has "peak experiences," there is often felt a desire for something more. In that regard, what was sought to fulfill this desire only served as a pointer to something beyond. To see this second premise requires honest introspection. Human history and great literature show that this experience of desire is universal. "The greatest of us who appreciate the greatest things the most are most discontent; we want something we cannot define, attain, or imagine attaining."

The second characteristic of the desire echoes Lewis's thoughts that the satisfaction of this desire is sought above all other satisfactions. In this regard, the desire is preferred, and itself *becomes* the desire. "The longing itself seems to come from another realm." Thus, the conclusion is concerned with that which corresponds to the desire: There must exist something more than time, earth, and all creatures that can satisfy this desire. That something more, or beyond, points to God.

The something more that the desire points to is an unknown X, but one whose "direction" is known. By direction, Kreeft means it is more "satisfiable" than all satisfactions. Since the desire is not satisfied with what is finite and partial, the object is therefore more, and infinitely more. Therefore, what is arrived at is something that can satisfy the demands of this desire forever. Something that "no eye has seen nor ear heard, nor the heart of man imagined," (I Cor. 2:9), in other words, the real God.

Of all the philosophical arguments for God's existence, this one (while certainly not the most intellectual or rational argument) strikes me as being the most plausible, as it speaks directly to that in us which we know intuitively, not just intellectually. It appeals to us in ways that purely academic proofs do not and cannot. It speaks to our soul, not our brain.

As I think about my own journey of faith, I have come to recognize that I desire more than just what "sound" theology has to say. It is so true that "deep calls to deep" as we see in that most existential Psalm 42, which begins: *"As a deer pants for flowing streams, so pants my soul for you oh God."* Thirst, hunger, craving—these are the real indicators of our place before God, not right theology, not conformity to the consensus opinions of our denomination, and certainly not how our fellow believers judge us based on our outward expressions of the faith.

The Journey Continues

Debbie and I have been settled into life in South Philly for about five years now. Until a year or two ago, activities revolving around helping to build a church community occupied much of my time, energy, and thought as I moved through the process of pursuing ordination. The prospect of becoming an ordained minister in Christ Church raised the kinds of questions that I have discussed in this book. Aside from the question of whether or not I would have proved to be qualified as a pastor—or whether or not I would have been able to sustain enough interest in the ordination requirements—in hindsight, my biggest question is whether I would have been theologically qualified, that is, whether I would have been able to fully affirm the theological underpinnings of my denomination, which I most certainly would have had to embrace wholeheartedly.

I worked through the process diligently and honestly until I recognized that it was not to be—that I couldn't continue to pursue a ministry goal that I could dedicate myself to in all honesty. The questions and doubts that I've talked about in this book arose in the process, at times very gradually, as I wrestled to overcome what seemed to be minor differences that I thought I could overcome. At other times it was blatantly obvious that my doubts were serious enough to distance me from the process that I had so energetically embraced earlier on. I had no choice but to deal with the doubts head-on. But now that pursuit of ordination is a thing of the past, I look forward to the dialogue that will follow as I proceed along the path of my own faith journey, as well as participating in the journeys of my family and friends. Is it hard to walk away from a religious identity and practice that sustained me and was so much a part of my life for so many years? You bet it is. As Rachel Evans expresses it so well:

> A lot of people think the hardest part about religious doubt is feeling Isolated from God. It's not . . . The hardest part about doubt is feeling isolated from your community. There's nothing quite like going through the motions of Christian life . . . while internally questioning the very beliefs that hold the entire culture together . . .[102]

In a 2015 interview, Rachel Evans said that a public expression of doubt was a hard place that had to be crossed and that there's a feeling of loneliness and alienation from friends when one starts to experience doubt (https://www.pbs.org/video/kost-alison-lebovitz-rachel-held-evans).   Like any other community, the church is a lifeline that embraces and supports us as a part of something bigger than ourselves, as something that we in that community share in common. The loss of that community is painful. But I believe it is also healing. The healing process is never without pain. It is an overcoming of the loss of health. It's a battle! But it's a necessary battle, and one that I am fully committed to fighting.

---

102. Rachel Evans, *Inspired: Slaying Giants, Walking on Water, and Loving the Bible Again* (Nashville, TN: Nelson Books/HarperCollins, 2018, page XXX.

Conclusion

G regory Boyd sums up what it is like for me to be on this journey. In the first chapter of his book *Benefit of the Doubt*—a chapter so appropriately titled "Embracing the Pain"—he talks about "how painful doubt can be when it concerns the things that matter the most to us—and there is nothing that matters more than the sense of identity, worth, purpose, and security that is associated with our faith."[103] I mentioned earlier that there is a cost to writing this book. I felt it when I started writing it, and I feel it even more now that I've finished it. It hasn't been an easy book to write. Along the way I found myself hesitating at many points to consider whether I should go on with certain lines of thought that might possibly be better left unwritten—ideas that brought into question some of my lifelong beliefs. To an extent, I still feel the urge to keep this to myself as a personal journal rather than putting it out there as a book. But in the end, I'm compelled to be unapologetic about what I have written. I didn't choose to explore the oddities and inconsistencies of my own faith. They are apparent, they can't be ignored, and very simply, there is too much at stake to be less than honest and open about them.

---

103. Gregory Boyd, *Benefit of the Doubt: Breaking the Idol of Certainty* (Ada, MI: Baker Books, 2013), page 31.

Since, as the subtitle of this book indicates, my journey is evolving, obviously this book hasn't resolved the journey. There may come a time when I write another book resolving my faith crisis, or even retracting some of what I've written in this book. If and when that happens, if the twists and turns of my personal journey lead me back toward my spiritual roots, I will gladly retract whatever needs to be retracted. I am sensible enough to recognize that the influences that shape an individual's faith evolve over a lifetime—that much is clear enough even from the very idea behind the phenomenon of conversion.

I also recognize that my journey is not the typical journey of other Christian believers, which is why I fully recognize that there will be repercussions from my own intimate circle of Christians. I also realize that life isn't static (thankfully). One must be honest enough to go to where the evidence takes one. That means *all* the evidence: literary and experiential, including evidence as it presents itself over time. One thing I've learned, from living in a damaged world; from my years of study in the world of biblical scholarship; and in general, from spending most of my adult life enmeshed in the two worlds of Judaism and Christianity: Biblical interpretation is a hazardous undertaking. That's why there are so many denominations in both the Christian and the Jewish faiths. As far as this book is concerned, the bottom line is that at the very minimum, I hope it will help you recognize, articulate, accept, and explore some of the questions that you might be asking in the privacy of your own thought life, and that it might give you the courage to dig deeper and more openly into those questions.

Beyond that, as for my own personal journey, I will hopefully remain open and energetic about pursuing the ongoing questions of faith that occupy my thinking. As I've grown older, I have noticed the beginnings of a tendency toward intellectual laziness (or perhaps more accurately, "selectivity") in pursuit of learning. It's interesting to look back and see how this has played out over the last decade or so. I'm no longer interested in the pursuit of dogmatic theology, that is, defense of the faith through the reinforcement of biblical theology. I have gotten rid of most of my scholarly books, narrowing down my personal library to those books (some old and some recently acquired) that speak to me about my journey of faith. Even though many of them just sit on my shelf, I like to see them and know that they're there in case I decide to go back to them, which I do from time to time. I'm attached to them, like a comfortable but worn-out chair or sweatshirt or pair of shoes. They represent a defiant quality in me, to hold on to my interest in pursuit of biblical knowledge (although waning as it is), to continue seeking after truth no matter how evasive, to pursue studying and learning, and most of all to continue in my faith journey, realizing (or perhaps better, hoping) that the journey will go on, maybe unresolved, until the day I finally see and understand the truth of all that matters on the other side.

Selected Writings

Following are a few examples of my writing through the years that best represent some important steps in my personal faith journey.

The thread becomes stronger

(Letter to the editor, published in *Biblical Archaeological Review*, 2007)

I wrote this letter several years after my graduate studies at Dropsie University, after I thought I had settled most of the questions of doubt that I write about in this book. But as I have made clear, in the years after I wrote this letter, I was never able to return completely to what we call in Evangelical circles the "childlike faith" that I had earlier in life. Here is the text of that letter:

> Thank you for publishing such a wonderful article on losing faith.
>
> As a former graduate student in Biblical Studies, I struggled for many years with the issues of faith expressed by these scholars, particularly Bart Ehrman and James Strange. Having been raised in an Evangelical Christian home and having studied at a Bible college,

I grew up accepting the Bible as literal, historical truth without question.

When I began to study the Bible critically, it was an enlightening experience. How quickly and easily in my first year of study I began to renounce [question] what I had, for 28 years, considered to be the absolute truth of Scripture. But even more surprising was the fact that it didn't bother me. Indeed, the heady experience of "becoming enlightened" overshadowed any guilt I may have felt as my grip on my lifelong faith quickly slipped away.

But I held on to my faith, if by a thread, for the sake of my family.

Although there were many years of internal struggle as I went through the motions of being a believer, I look back today—23 years later—with a thankful heart that I did not follow the path that would have led me to abandon my faith.

Faith requires overcoming what is not evident empirically. If the existence of God could be proved, it would not require faith.

As I read this letter again, 13 years after I wrote it, I still have not abandoned my faith, yet I don't think I can state that last line quite as unoquivically as I did back then. As you have seen from reading this book, now I simply don't know if my faith is strong enough to withstand the absence of empirical evidence.

Ruth and hesed *June, 2011*

This piece represents my attachment to the idea of God as a being who expresses a deeper and stronger love than I can ever imagine. I've always loved the biblical idea of the *hesed* of God, as it represents an ideal for me of what I most desire God to be like, whether I see Him that way or not . . .

One of the most painfully obvious differences between ancient Israelite and modern Western culture is the loss of the concept and practice of covenant community. All civilizations up to recent times have experienced meaningful community, both familial and societal. Only in recent history have we lost the idea of community and become a society of individuals, who—although living in a world full of people all around us—are alone. Loneliness is an epidemic in our world today.

Perhaps the most meaningful word in the Hebrew Bible (the Old Testament) is a word that expresses better than any other word the idea of community: the word *hesed* (pronounced *chesed*), translated by the King James Bible as "loving kindness," and in other translations as "kindness," "faithfulness," "steadfast love," "mercy," and so on. The central meaning of this word is the idea of reciprocal kindness between two parties who are in covenant relationship with each other.

The word appears in many narratives in the Old Testament, but one of the most vivid illustrations of the idea of *hesed* is in the story of Ruth. The Book of Ruth is a love story that interrupts the narrative of the history of Israel, a history characterized by war, disloyalty, wicked kings, family disputes, murders, and more. And in the midst of all this turmoil, we have the story of a romance that begins in a foreign country and ends back in the land of Israel, and in fact provides the background for the future salvation of Israel.

Naomi, an Israelite living in the land of Moab, suffers the loss of her husband and her two sons, and is left alone with her two daughters-in-law (Moabite women who married Naomi's two sons). Left without protection and bereaved by her great loss, she decides to return to Bethlehem, her homeland. One of her daughters-in-law decides to remain in her own homeland, Moab. But the other, Ruth, refuses to part with her mother-in-law, and in fact becomes attached (literally "glued" or "stuck") to Naomi (Ruth 1:14). In one of the most moving passages of Scripture, Ruth responds to Naomi's desire to release her with the words: *"Where you go I will go, and where you lodge I will lodge. Your people shall be my people and your God my God. Where you die I will die, and there will I be buried."*

The key to our understanding of Ruth's and Naomi's newly formed covenant relationship is found in 1:8. Encouraging Ruth and Orpah to go back to their homes, Naomi says: "May the Lord show you kindness *(hesed)* as you have shown me." Ruth's refusal to abandon Naomi, her pledge to stay with her through thick and thin, her "clinging" to Naomi, is a wonderfully vivid picture of the *hesed* relationship. Ruth has bound herself to Naomi in a covenant relationship at the cost of leaving behind her life in her homeland and going to a strange land.

Toward the end of the narrative, when Boaz (Naomi's relative) is introduced into the story, again we see the act of kindness *(hesed)* shown first by Boaz to Ruth (2:20) in allowing her to gather food from his field under his protection, then from Ruth to Boaz (3:10). In this last incident, we see not only the romantic outcome of these reciprocal acts of kindness, but (much more importantly) we are introduced to the deeper meaning of the *hesed* relationship—that of the Redeemer on behalf of the redeemed (Chapter 4), *a so-called kinsman redeemer.* Out of this *hesed* relationship between Boaz and Ruth comes a son, "Obed, who was the father of Jesse, the father of David" (4:17). And the story continues, as a future descendant would come in that same lineage about 1,000 years later, who would be our Messiah and who would show us the greatest act of *hesed* by giving His own life in our place to redeem us from our sins.

Did God become less than God? November 2011

In this article, published in *Papyrus Prose,* I write about my understanding of what it must have taken for God to condescend to care for His fallen creation. I remember being struck with a sense of awe over the generosity of a God who sets aside, or "constricts," his greatness in order to relate to his created beings.

During a recent discussion with my colleague and former teacher, we talked about the Jewish view of the Sabbath day as a holy day. He said that to an observing Jew, the holiness of the Sabbath goes even beyond the Day of Atonement (Yom Kippur), which most Jews consider to be the holiest day. Why is every Sabbath day even holier than Yom Kippur, which occurs only once a year and is considered by many Jews to be the holiest day of the Jewish year? Because the Sabbath is the one day of the week that belongs *exclusively* to God. The Sabbath is to be a day full of joy, when God is thought to be present with humankind. On the Sabbath day, God, in a real sense, actually condescends ("comes down") to humans, to be intimately near his people Israel.

But how can God, being wholly above and outside of humanity, come into the world of humanity unless He becomes less than who He is—less than God? How can the Creator come down to the level of his creation? Judaism holds that God is so high above man, so distinct and distant from man, that His name cannot even be uttered. Thus an orthodox Jew would never vocalize the name YHWH (commonly vocalized as Jehovah), but when reading or quoting from the Scriptures, he would read *"The Name"* or *"The Lord"* in place of YHWH. Not only can a Jew not refer to God using His personal name, but in fact, God cannot even be described accurately using the conventional pronouns "He," "Him," or even "the Lord," since He is so far above and outside of humanity.

Biblical Hebrew does not contain vowels. Rather, correct vocalization is established by vowel letters. It is interesting that the personal name of Israel's God is made up of three Hebrew vowel letters YHWH, with no consonants. Therefore, the name, as it was pronounced by the ancient Israelites, cannot be known. Even when spelling the word "God," an observing Jew will spell it "G-d" so as not to profane the name.

So how does Holy God, who is so far above His created world, whose name is so holy that it cannot even cross the lips of a Jew, how can such a God come down to humanity as He is believed to do on the Sabbath?

The Old Testament makes abundantly clear the vast distance between humanity and God. When Moses approached Mount Sinai to receive the Ten Commandments, the people were strictly warned not to go near the mountain or they would be struck dead (Exodus 19:9–13). Moses's permission to approach God on the mountain is clearly an exception to the rule. As we learn from the story of the Golden Calf (Exodus 32:11–14 and 30–35),

Moses was commissioned by God with a special role as intercessor between God and the Israelites.

But even Moses could not see God's face. Let's look at that fascinating story in Exodus 33–34, where Moses experiences the impossible—he is actually permitted to see God as no one before him or after him has been allowed to do. Faced with the overwhelming burden of leading the Israelites to freedom, Moses asks God to ". . . show me your way, that I may know you." God assures Moses that He would go with him, literally "My face [presence) will go with you" (33:14), to which Moses responds: "If your presence does not go with me, do not bring us up from here" (v. 15). God agrees to Moses's request, and Moses then dares to make a further plea for God to "show me your glory" (v. 18), to which God responds: "I will cause to pass before you all of my goodness."

What we see in this exchange between Moses and God is nothing short of amazing: God condescends to share with Moses something that He has not up to this point in human history revealed—His presence in the form of His glory and His goodness. And how is God going to reveal Himself to Moses? By passing before Moses and simply speaking His own name "YHWH" as He passes by. And while it is true that God's "face" would "go with Moses" as we saw in v. 14, we see here, in v. 20, that Moses is not permitted to actually see God's face as He passes by.

So, God condescends to reveal Himself to his chosen servant Moses, who acts as intercessor between God and Israel. But this still doesn't adequately explain how the holy God, the King of the Universe, can stoop to the level of His created beings to commune with them each Sabbath day. Even earthly kings do not humble themselves to the level of their subjects. How much more the King of Kings, the eternal God? Trying to understand how much greater God is than his creation in human language is impossible. As Peter Kreeft has described it, the distance between a man and an animal is vast, but still discernable. The distance between humans and one-celled amoebas is even more distant, but still understandable. In fact, the distance between a man and an inanimate object is still more vast, but not yet inestimable. But the distance between God and humanity is infinite.

According to the Kabbalah (mystical study in Hebrew thought), the best way to describe God's condescendence to humankind, although grossly inadequate, is that He comes down to humans by making Himself less than what He is, by "constricting" or narrowing down His divine essence to the point where He can be present with man. The Hebrew word that describes this narrowing process is *tsimtsum*, meaning "retraction." According to this idea, God was alone in eternity. There was no other existence, only His presence, which occupied all of space (as we understand the idea of space). His first act of *tsimtsum* (retracting His presence) was the act of Creation, where He in effect decreased His presence in space by bringing into existence created beings.

This is not to imply that God's presence and being became any less when He created. His act of Creation, as well as His subsequent benevolent acts on behalf of His creatures, do not lessen His essence. And His creative act and His involvement with His created beings are superfluous to His being—they in no way make God more complete or "better off."

This Hebrew thought process is difficult to capture and comprehend, because we are still left with the question: *How* does He do it? How does He bridge the distance between Himself and His creation so that on each Sabbath His real presence is with humanity? Judaism's mystical explanation of God coming down to man of course does not adequately explain *how* He condescends to enter into such a personal relationship with His creation, only that He *does*. And although the Old Testament (Hebrew Bible) hints here and there that there would come a time when God would reveal Himself to man in fuller and more personal way, the Hebrew Scriptures leave us waiting and hoping for that future day when the messiah would come and restore humankind with the Creator.

Of course, Philippians 2 gives us an answer: *"Being in the form of God . . . he was made in the likeness of man."* How else could divinity reach down to humanity, how else could the Creator reach down to creation, how could God stoop down to meet with humans, except through Him becoming one of His own creatures? By coming down to the level of humankind as a man, God (so to speak) constricted Himself, narrowed down His essence to the point where other men could see him, His parents could raise Him from a baby, His friends could play, eat, and drink with him, and His enemies could persecute him and finally kill him. And this is the mystery of the incarnation—God condescended to make Himself as one of His creatures, less than who He is, while never *becoming* less than who He is.

Abraham's sacrifice of Isaac: "nonrational" but not "irrational"

This article (published in *Papyrus Prose* in 2012) is a reflection on Søren Kierkegaard's expression of the "paradox of faith," an idea that continually resonates with me.

One of the most dramatic—and disturbing—stories in the Book of Genesis, the Binding of Isaac (22:1–14) is introduced by the phrase: "After these events," suggesting some sort of connection between this account of Abraham's offering of Isaac and events in Abraham's life that led up to his sacrifice of Isaac. What were those events that precede this account, and what background can they provide for helping us better understand its profound meaning and message?

Two seemingly unrelated stories precede the story of the sacrifice of Isaac: The first story (21:1–21) is the account of the birth and early years of Isaac. In this narrative, Ishmael, the son of Sarah's slave woman, is now a young boy. After waiting for so many years for the promised son, when Abraham is 100 years old, he and Sarah (at age 90) finally have the promised son, Isaac. At a feast given by Abraham celebrating Isaac's weaning, a dispute arises between Sarah and Hagar over the status of their sons Isaac and Ishmael, resulting in the banishment of Hagar and Ishmael from the family and Isaac's status as Abraham's sole heir. We get a strong sense of the callousness of Sarah and Abraham in this act, until we are told that God Himself initiated the expulsion.

The second story (21:22–34) revolves around a dispute between Abraham and Abimelech (king of a neighboring Philistine city) over a plot of real estate, resulting in Abraham's acquisition of a portion of land that would later become Israel's southern border.

These two events serve to give the impression that Abraham and his family have reached a state of settlement, security, and stability. After so many years of waiting, he has the son God had promised, he is living in peace with neighboring communities, and he is finally able to settle into a life of relative comfort and happiness.

But God has other plans. He is not content to allow Abraham, His chosen servant, to live out the rest of his life in obscurity, for He has yet to teach Abraham (and through Abraham, us) the greatest lesson, indeed the central message of all Scripture: *what it means to sacrifice everything for the sake of obedience and devotion to God.* It is true that Abraham had displayed great faith in leaving his country so many years prior, and trusting God to sustain him in a hostile foreign land to which He brought him and especially in not losing hope through the long years of not seeing the promise of a son fulfilled.

But Abraham is about to experience the ultimate test of love for God: *obedience in the face of apparent irrationality.* In all the commentary and writing on this biblical story, no one has been able to express the natural reaction of horror, even revulsion, that we all feel when reading this story better than Christian philosopher Søren Kierkegaard. In his famous book, *Fear and Trembling,* Kierkegaard expresses the inner conflict that we all sense Abraham must have experienced when God dramatically placed this challenge before him. Kierkegaard comments: "Though Abraham arouses my admiration, he at the same time appalls me." His reaction is not surprising, and if we are to be honest, it is not unlike the reaction we all must feel when we read this story. Kierkegaard is, at the same time, repulsed but also awed by such a demand placed by God on His chosen servant. He sees this act of Abraham as "a giving up of the finite in order to grasp the infinite" and characterizes it as an act of "infinite resignation."

Everything about this story strikes us as irrational: First God honors His word by giving Abraham the son whom He had been promising for so many years—then He tells him to kill him. Abraham obeys without a moment's hesitation, with not even a question or demand for an explanation. In every respect, this seems to be an irrational and senseless demand on God's part, and an irrational response on the part of Abraham. How does one understand such a seeming absurdity? In Kierkegaard's words, ". . . movements of faith must constantly be made by virtue of the absurd." Faith, to Kierkegaard, is a paradox. *One can only keep what he can truly renounce.* In the words of Jesus, recorded by Matthew: "He who finds his life will lose it, and he who loses his life for my sake will find it."

So if we are honest in our reaction to this story, we must see it as irrational. But let's not mistake the *irrational* for the *nonrational*. There is a big difference. Irrationality implies stupidity, folly, lack of common sense. But to be nonrational implies an act of the will—a choice—to put aside the action that seems to make more sense or seems more reasonable in favor of a better choice. God places a clear choice before Abraham: "You can demonstrate your supreme love and devotion to me by sacrificing what you love most— the life of your son. Or keep your son and thereby demonstrate that you refuse to obey me unconditionally—certainly an irrational demand and an impossible choice for God to place on a mere human. One can imagine and relate to Abraham's inner conflict: *Why can't I hold onto the son that you had been promising me for so many years and finally gave me, and at the same time maintain my love and devotion to you?* While Abraham doesn't openly question God, we can only imagine the extent of his internal anguish over the seeming absurdity of such an offensive directive from God.

If we were to read this story for the first time without any preconceptions of how Abraham might react, we would say: "Obviously Abraham will do the right thing—question God and argue that it is out of God's character to demand such a thing." We would expect him to reason with God, reminding Him of His past promises and final fulfillment of His word. But to our amazement, Abraham does obey God, and without a moment's hesitation. As they approach their destination and Abraham instructs his servants to stay behind, we read that *". . . the two of them* [Abraham and Isaac] *walked on together,"* a startling picture of complete solidarity of father and son as they conclude their fateful journey together, in complete unity, toward a trial so horrific that we are tempted (like Kierkegaard) to be repulsed by the impossibility of such a scene.

Of course this story is a clear foreshadowing of God's sacrifice of His be-loved son. And in both stories the reaction of revulsion is exactly the nat-ural reaction, the appropriate reaction. For here we come face to face with life's ultimate question: How can a father, who loves his only son with so great a love, kill that son? There is no word to describe it but "irrational." And while Abraham doesn't openly question God, we can only imagine the extent of his internal anguish over the seeming absurdity of such an odious directive.

Likewise, how can we begin to imagine the extent of God's anguish over His sacrifice of His only son, Jesus? And in fact, our confusion is height-ened by the added revelation that no one demanded that sacrifice of God. He was both the initiator of the decision and the executioner. Further-more, Jesus, like Isaac, went willingly in cooperation with his father. But unlike Isaac, whose comprehension of what his father was about to do was somewhat hidden from his understanding, Jesus not only submitted to His father's will in going to the cross, but He participated, in full agreement with His father's will from eternity past. So that what seems to be, in every respect, an irrational event, we now recognize as something completely different: a *nonrational* but divine decision, an agreement, in the mind of the eternal God—Father, Son, and Holy Spirit—with eternal significance for humankind. An event that at first seems to our frail minds to be an act so senseless, so meaningless, becomes perfectly clear as the loving act of a sovereign God who uses extraordinary means to bring about the salvation of His creation.

Bibliography

Berger, Peter. "The Good of Religious Pluralism." In *First Things,* April 2016, page 42. https://www.firstthings.com/article/2016/04/the-good-of-religious-pluralism

Berger, Peter. *In Praise of Doubt: How to Have Convictions without Becoming a Fanatic.* New York: HarperCollins, 2009.

Berkouwer, G. C. *Divine Election.* Grand Rapids, MI: Eerdmans Publishing, 1960.

Boyd, Gregory A. *Benefit of the Doubt: Breaking the Idol of Certainty.* Ada, MI: Baker Books, 2013.

Boyd, Gregory A. *The God of the Possible: A Biblical Introduction to the Open View of God.* Ada, MI: Baker Books, 2000.

Buechner, Frederick. *The Sacred Journey: A Memoir of Early Days.* New York: HarperCollins, 1982.

Calvin, John. *Institutes of the Christian Religion.* (various editions).

Cox, Harvey. *The Future of Faith* (New York: HarperCollins, 2009).

Daane, James. *The Freedom of God: A Study of Election and Pulpit.* Grand Rapids, MI: Eerdmans Publishing, 2015.

Davies, Alan. *Antisemitism and the Foundations of Christianity.* Mahwah, NJ: Paulist Press, 1979.

Dostoevsky, Fyodor. *The Brothers Karamazov.* New York: Farrar, Straus and Giroux, 1990.

Dubay, Thomas. *Faith and Certitude: Can We Be Sure of the Things that Matter Most to Us?* San Francisco: Ignatius Press, 1985.

DeYoung, Kevin. *Taking God at His Word: Why the Bible Is Knowable, Necessary, and Enough, and What That Means for You and Me.* Wheaton, IL: Crossway, 2014.

Eliade, Mircea. *The Sacred and the Profane: The Nature of Religion.* New York: Harcourt, Brace, & Co., 1959.

Evans, Rachel. *Inspired: Slaying Giants, Walking on Water, and Loving the Bible Again.* Nashville, TN: Nelson Books/HarperCollins, 2018.

Evans, Rachel. *Searching for Sunday: Loving, Leaving, and Finding the Church.* Nashville, TN: Nelson Books/HarperCollins, 2015.

Frankl, Viktor. *The Will to Meaning: Foundations and Applications of Logotherapy.* New York: Penguin Books, 1969.

Frankl, Victor. *Man's Search for Meaning.* New York: Penguin Books, 1968.

Gager, John. *The Origins of Antisemitism: Attitudes Toward Judaism in Pagan and Christian Antiquity.* London: Oxford University Press, 1983.

Gay, Doug. *Remixing the Church: Towards an Emerging Ecclesiology.* London: SCM Press, 2011.

Goldman, Robert N. *Einstein's God: Albert Einstein's Quest As a Scientist and As a Jew to Replace a Forsaken God.* Lanham, MD: Jason Aronson, Inc., 1997.

Guardini, Romano. *The Faith and Modern Man.* New York: Pantheon Books, 1952.

Holloway, Richard. *Crossfire: Faith and Doubt in an Age of Uncertainty.* Grand Rapids, MI: Eerdmans Publishing, 1988.

Holloway, Richard. *Dancing on the Edge: Faith in a Post-Christian Age.* New York: HarperCollins, 1997.

Holloway, Richard. *Doubts and Loves: What is Left of Christianity.* Edinburgh, UK: Canongate Books Ltd., 2001.

Holloway, Richard. *Godless Morality.* Edinburgh, UK: Canongate Books, 1999.

Howard-Snyder, Daniel & Moser, Paul (Eds.). *Divine Hiddenness: New Essays.* Cambridge, UK: Cambridge University Press, 2002.

Kearney, Richard. *Anatheism: Returning to God after God.* New York: Columbia University Press, 2011.

Kreeft, Peter. *Jesus Shock.* South Bend, IN: St. Augustine's Press, 2008.

Kreeft, Peter. *Love is Stronger than Death.* San Francisco: Ignatius Press, 1979.

Kreeft, Peter. *Making Choices: Practical Wisdom for Everyday Moral Decisions.* Ann Arbor, MI: Servant Books, 1990.

Kullberg, Kelly Monroe. *Finding God Beyond Harvard: The Quest for Veritas.* Downers Grove, IL: IVP Books, 2006.

Küng, Hans. *On Being a Christian.* New York: Doubleday, 1976.

Lewis, C. S., "On Obstinacy and Belief" In: *The World's Last Night.* New York: Harcourt Brace & Co., 1988, pages 13–30.

Lewis, C. S., *The Pilgrim's Regress.* Ann Arbor, MI: Eerdmans Publishing, 1943.

Lewis, C. S. *Surprised by Joy: The Shape of My Early Life.* New York: Harcourt Brace & Co., 1955.

Marcel, Gabriel. *Being and Having.* London: Dacre Press, 1949.

McLaren, Brian. *Everything Must Change: Jesus, Global Crisis, and a Revolution of Hope.* Nashville, TN: Thomas Nelson, 2007.

McLaren, Brian. *A Generous Orthodoxy: Why I am a Missional, Evangelical, Post/Protestant, Liberal/Conservative, Biblical, Charismatic/Contemplative, Fundamentalist/Calvinist, Anabaptist/Anglican, Methodist, Catholic, Green, Incarnational, Depressed-Yet-Hopeful, Emergent, Unfinished Christian.* Grand Rapids, MI: Zondervan Publishing, 2004.

McLaren, Brian. *A Search for What Makes Sense: Finding Faith.* Grand Rapids, MI: Zondervan Publishing, 1999.

McLaren, Brian. *Finding Faith: A Self-Discovery Guide for Your Spiritual Quest.* Grand Rapids, MI: Zondervan Publishing, 1999.

Metaxas, Eric (Ed.). *Socrates in the City: Conversations on "Life, God, and Other Small Topics."* New York: Dutton, 2011.

Miller, Ronald. *Dialogue and Disagreement: Franz Rosenzweig's Relevance to Contemporary Jewish-Christian Understanding.* Lanham, MD: University Press of America, 1990.

Miller, Donald E. *Reinventing American Protestantism: Christianity in the New Millennium.* Berkeley, CA: University of California Press, 1997.

Nouwen, Henry. *Reaching Out: The Three Movements of the Spiritual Life.* New York: Doubleday, 1986.

Olson, Roger E. *Against Calvinism: Rescuing God's Reputation from Radical Reformed Theology.* Grand Rapids, MI: Zondervan Publishing, 2011.

Otto, Rudolf. *The Idea of the Holy: An Inquiry into the Non-rational Factor in the Idea of the Divine and its Relation to the Rational.* New York: Oxford University Press, 1958.

Peck, Scott. *The Road Less Traveled.* New York: Simon & Schuster, 1978.

Piper, John. "God Does Not Repent Like a Man," https://www.desiringgod.org/articles/god-does-not-repent-like-a-man

Piper, John. "What Made it Okay for God to Kill Women and Children in the Old Testament?" https://www.desiringgod.org/interviews/what-made-it-okay-for-god-to-kill-women-and-children-in-the-old-testament

Robinson, A. T. *Honest to God.* Philadelphia: Westminster Press, 1953.

Rohr, Richard. https://cac.org/my-own-journey-2019-03-25/

Ruether, Rosemary. *Disputed Questions: On Being a Christian.* Ossining, NY: Orbis Books, 1989.

Ruether, Rosemary. *Faith and Fratricide: The Theological Roots of Anti-Semitism.* New York: Seabury Press, 1974.

Strobel, Lee. *The Case for Faith: A Journalist Investigates the Toughest Objections to Christianity.* Grand Rapids, MI: Zondervan Publishing, 2008.

Sweeney, Jon M. *Inventing Hell: Dante, the Bible, and Eternal Torment.* Nashville, TN: Jericho Books, 2014.

Tillich, Paul. *The Courage to Be.* New Haven, CT: Yale University Press, 1980.

Tillich, Paul. *The New Being.* New York: Charles Scribner's Sons, 1955.

Tournier, Paul. *Learn To Grow Old.* New York: Harper & Row, 1972.

Tournier, Paul. *The Adventure of Living.* New York: Harper & Row, 1965.

Vattimo, Gianni. *After Christianity.* New York: Columbia University Press, 2002.

Witherington, Ben. *The Problem with Evangelical Theology: Testing the Exegetical Foundations of Calvinism, Dispensationalism, Wesleyanism, and Pentecostalism.* Waco, TX: Baylor University Press, 2016.